# THE

# COMPLETE

# LEGAL KIT

Over 150 Ready-To-Use Legal Forms & Agreements to Protect You

Your Family, Your Home and Your Business

**Consumer Law Foundation**

New York, New York

Running Press
Philadelphia, Pennsylvania

Canadian representatives: General Publishing Co., Ltd.,
30 Lesmill Road, Don Mills, Ontario M3B 2T6.
International representatives: Worldwide Media Services, Inc.,
115 East Twenty-third Street, New York, NY 10010.

9 8 7 6 5 4 3 2 1
Digit on the right indicates the number of this printing.

ISBN 0-89471-613-1
Cover design by Toby Schmidt.

The Consumer Law Foundation is a national organization formed
to make legal information more readily available to the public
through seminars, books, self-help manuals, and other instruc-
tional aids. Through its efforts, countless Americans have gained
affordable access to basic information on everyday legal matters.
The Consumer Law Foundation also has developed *The Complete
Family Record Organizer.*

*The Complete Legal Kit* and *The Complete Family Record
Organizer* may be ordered by mail from the publisher.
Please include $1.50 postage for each book. *But try your
bookstore first!*
Running Press Book Publishers
125 South Twenty-second Street
Philadelphia, Pennsylvania 19103

# THE COMPLETE LEGAL KIT

**The Complete Legal Kit** is a valuable one-of-a-kind portfolio of agreements and legal forms to protect you, your family, your home and your business from everyday legal problems.

With over 150 vital legal documents in all, you now have at your fingertips the protection you need without the expense and inconvenience of relying on an attorney for routine legal matters.

From contracts to affidavits, from bills of sale to living wills, **The Complete Legal Kit** carefully documents your important transactions, helps you avoid disputes and everyday legal problems, and provides the ideal way to "get it in writing" and protect your valuable rights. Within seconds you can have precisely the document you need to eliminate costly misunderstandings and expensive lawsuits, comply with complex legal requirements and safely bypass personal and corporate liability.

Prepared by a distinguished panel of lawyers and law professors, **The Complete Legal Kit** offers you the safest, most efficient and most economical way to handle everyday legal matters. For pennies you have the very same documents that could easily cost $100 or more from a lawyer. Think of the hundreds, perhaps thousands, of dollars you can save each year on legal fees.

Valid and enforceable in all 50 states, you will find the forms amazingly easy to use. Every form is written in concise, simple to follow language for proper use.

## HOW TO USE THE
## COMPLETE LEGAL KIT

You can conveniently use **The Complete Legal Kit** by following these step-by-step instructions:

1. To find the appropriate form for your purpose check the table of contents. You may find several forms for the same purpose so compare and select the one that best meets your needs.

2. Each form is perforated for easy removal. Photocopy the original so it can be stored for repeated use.

3. Fully complete each form. Make certain all names, dates, amounts and other blanks on the form are filled in (or deleted, if inapplicable). Add all other agreed upon terms to the document together with any other modification that reflects the agreement between the parties. Attach a rider to the form if additional terms cannot be conveniently added to the original. Important changes or riders should be initialled by all parties to acknowledge the change. Remember, verbal terms may not be binding, so be certain the document properly includes all that was agreed upon.

4.        The forms can be easily modified or customized to your special needs, and correspondence forms can be easily personalized by reproducing them on your own letterhead.

5.        Signatures on the form should indicate the roles of the parties signing. For example, if the signer is a corporation it may be signed: XYZ Corp. by John Jones, President.

6.        Several of the forms have specific instructions which are footnoted. The footnotes are there because they offer important additional instructions on the proper use of the form and should therefore be followed closely.

7.        The forms in this book frequently use the pronoun "it" to refer to a given party. It is acceptable to use "it" in place of "his" or "her" when referring to a natural person so no change is required. Further, "it" is the appropriate pronoun to designate a corporation, partnership or any other legal entity.

8.        Important notices and correspondence should always be delivered by certified mail, return receipt requested, so that you have proof of delivery.

9.        **The Complete Legal Kit** has been prepared by a panel of attorneys who agree the forms are generally appropriate for self-use. Nevertheless, as with any legal matter, use common sense to decide when you should seek professional legal advice rather than rely on these forms or any other do-it-yourself legal forms. Always consult your attorney to draft complex or important agreements, and for transactions involving substantial amounts of money, or for any matter where you don't understand the proper use of a form or question its adequacy to protect you. Because we cannot in any way be certain that the forms in this kit are being properly used, we cannot assume liability or responsibility for their incorrect use.

# CONTENTS

## 1 REAL ESTATE

## 2 LEASES AND TENANCIES

# 3   EMPLOYMENT

# 4   CREDIT AND COLLECTIONS

# 5    LOANS AND DEBTS

# 6    SALE OR PERSONAL PROPERTY

# 9  OTHER LEGAL FORMS

# REAL ESTATE

1

# PURCHASE OPTION AGREEMENT

Purchase Option Agreement by and between

(Owner) and                                                    (Buyer).

1.      Buyer hereby pays to Owner the sum of $                    in consideration

for this option, which option payment shall _____ shall not _____ be credited to the

purchase price if the option is exercised.

2.      Buyer has the option and right to buy



(property) during the option period for the full price of $

3.      This option will remain in effect from this date to                    , 19        ,

and thereupon expire unless sooner exercised.

4.      To exercise the option, Buyer must notify Owner of same by certified mail within

the option period.

5.      Should Buyer exercise the option, then Buyer and Owner shall sign the attached

and completed contract of sale within            days thereafter, and consummate the sale

on its terms.

6.      This option agreement shall be binding upon and inure to the benefit of the

parties, their successors, assigns and personal representatives.

Signed under seal this            day of                    , 19      .

In the presence of:


_____          _____
                                           Owner


_____          _____
                                           Buyer

# REAL ESTATE BROKERAGE AGREEMENT

1.      This brokerage agreement entered into on the              day of                      ,

19        , by and between                                          (Owner) and

                              (Real Estate Broker) who agree as follows:

2.      Listing term: Owner lists the property described in Paragraph 3, with the Real

Estate Broker for a period of                      days, commencing on this date.

3.      Description of Property: The property to be listed is located and described as:




4.      Commission: The Owner agrees to pay the Real Estate Broker a commission of

        % of the sale price if the Broker finds a purchaser ready, willing, and able to pay at

least $                      for the property or such other sum as may be accepted by Owner,

said commission payable only upon closing.

5.      Non-Exclusive: The Owner retains the right to sell the property directly with no

sales commission, so long as the Broker did not find this purchaser.  The Owner further

has the right to list the property with other brokers.  If a sale is made to parties introduced

by the Real Estate Agent within                      months after this agreement terminates, the

Owner shall pay the commission specified above.  Nothing herein is intended to create an

exclusive agency or exclusive right to sell.

6.      Forfeit of Deposit: If a deposit of money is forfeited by a purchaser, one-half shall

be retained by the Broker, providing that this amount does not exceed the commission,

and one-half shall be paid to the Owner.

7.      Termination: This agreement may be terminated by Owner at any time and the

property withdrawn from sale.

In the presence of:


_____        _____
                                        Owner


_____        _____
                                        Broker

# OFFER TO PURCHASE
# REAL ESTATE

BE IT KNOWN, the undersigned Buyer offers to purchase from

(Owner) real estate known as                                             , City/Town

of                              , County of                    , State of

said property more particularly described as:


and containing                      square feet of land.

        The purchase price is         $
        Deposit herewith paid        $
        Upon signing sales agreement   $
        Balance at closing           $_____
            Total purchase price      $

This offer is subject to Buyer obtaining a real estate mortgage for no less than

$                     payable over            years with interest not to exceed          %  at

customary terms within              days from date hereof.

This offer is further subject to Buyer obtaining a satisfactory home inspection

report and termite/pest report within                days from date hereof.

Seller shall pay                                        (Broker) a commission of

$                          upon closing.

Said property is to be sold free and clear of all encumbrances, by good and

marketable title, with full possession of said property available to Buyer.

The parties agree to execute a standard purchase and sales agreement on the

terms contained within              days.

The closing shall be on or before                               , 19          , at the

deed recording office.

Signed under seal this                day of                          , 19


_____    _____
Broker                                   Buyer

                                     _____
                                     Owner

# ESCROW AGREEMENT

AGREEMENT between                                        (Seller),

(Buyer) and

(Escrow Agent).

Simultaneously with the making of this Agreement, Seller and Buyer have

entered into a contract (the Contract) by which Seller will sell to Buyer the following

property:

The closing will take place on                              , 19      , at            a.m.,

at the offices of                                                   , located at

                                                                or at such

other time and place as Seller and Buyer may jointly designate in writing.  Pursuant to the

Contract, Buyer must deposit $                              as a down payment to be held in

escrow by Escrow Agent.

The $                              down payment referred to hereinabove has been

paid by Buyer to Escrow Agent.  Escrow Agent acknowledges receipt of $

from Buyer by check, subject to collection.

If the closing takes place under the Contract, Escrow Agent at the time of closing

shall pay the amount deposited with him to Seller or in accordance with Seller's written

instructions.  Escrow Agent shall make simultaneous transfer of the said property to the

Buyer.

If no closing takes place under the Contract, Escrow Agent shall continue to hold

the amount deposited with him until he receives written authorization for its disposition

signed by both Buyer and Seller.  If there is any dispute as to whom Escrow Agent is to

deliver the amount deposited, Escrow Agent shall hold the sum until the parties' rights are

finally determined in an appropriate action or proceeding or until a court orders Escrow

Agent to deposit the down payment with it.  If Escrow Agent does not receive a proper written authorization from Seller and Buyer, or if an action or proceeding to determine

Seller's and Buyer's rights is not begun or diligently prosecuted, Escrow Agent is under

no obligation to bring an action or proceeding to deposit the sum held by him in court, but

may continue to hold the deposit.

Escrow Agent assumes no liability except that of a stakeholder. Escrow Agent's

duties are limited to those specifically set out in this Agreement. Escrow Agent shall incur

no liability to anyone except for willful misconduct or gross negligence so long as the

Escrow Agent acts in good faith. Seller and Buyer release Escrow Agent from any act

done or omitted in good faith in the performance of Escrow Agent's duties.


_____
Seller


_____     _____
Escrow Agent                          Buyer

# QUITCLAIM DEED

BE IT KNOWN, that                                                                              ,
Grantors of                                                    , County of                                    ,
State of                                , hereby QUITCLAIM and transfer to
                    , of                                        , County of                                    ,
State of                              , for the sum of $                          , the following described
land located in                                        County, State of                                , with
QUITCLAIM COVENANTS, to wit:

Being the same property conveyed to Grantors by deed of
                    , dated                                    , 19        .

WITNESS the hands of said Grantors this                    day of                                    ,
19        .

_____

_____

State of
                                      , SS.
County of                                                                                      , 19        .

Then personally appeared                                                                      ,
who acknowledged the foregoing, before me.

_____
Notary Public

My Commission Expires:

# WARRANTY DEED

BE IT KNOWN, that                                                    ,
Grantors, of                                              , County of                        ,
State of                              , hereby bargain, deed and convey to
          Grantee, of                                              , County of
          , State of                            , and his heirs and assigns, for the sum
of $                          , the following described land in                        County,
State of                              , free and clear with WARRANTY COVENANTS; to wit:

And Grantor, for himself and his heirs, hereby covenants with Grantee, his heirs, and assigns, that Grantor is lawfully seised in fee simple of the above-described premises; that he has a good right to convey; that the premises are free from all encumbrances; that Grantor and his heirs, and all persons acquiring any interest in the property granted, through or for Grantor, will, on demand of Grantee, or his heirs or assigns, and at the expense of Grantee, his heirs or assigns, execute any instrument necessary for the further assurance of the title to the premises that may be reasonably required; and that Grantor and his heirs will forever warrant and defend all of the property so granted to Grantee, his heirs, and assigns, against every person lawfully claiming the same or any part thereof.

Being the same property conveyed to the Grantors by deed of
                    , dated                              , 19        .

WITNESS the hands of said Grantors this                day of                              ,
19

_____

_____

State of
                        , SS.
County of                                                              , 19        .

Then personally appeared                                                          ,
who acknowledged the foregoing, before me.

_____
Notary Public

My Commission Expires:

# GRANT DEED

GRANT DEED made on                              , 19      , by
              , of                                                      , Grantor, to
                                             , of
              , Grantee.

Grantor, in consideration of $                        paid by Grantee, does hereby
grant to Grantee, his heirs and assigns, all that land lying in                                               ,
County of                              , State of                              , and bounded and
described as follows:

together with all the tenements, hereditaments, and appurtenances thereto belonging,
and the reversions, remainders, rents, issues, and profits, if any, thereof.

Executed at                                                      on the date first
above written.

_____

State of
                              , SS.
County of                                                                              , 19      .

Then personally appeared
who acknowledged the foregoing, before me.

_____
Notary Public

My Commission Expires:

# DISCHARGE OF MORTGAGE

BE IT KNOWN, for value received, we

, of

holders of a certain real estate mortgage from

to                                                    , said mortgage dated

19      , and recorded in Book or Volume                    , Page                    , of the

County Registry of Deeds, acknowledge full satisfaction and discharge of

same.

Signed under seal this          day of                              , 19      .

_____

_____

State of

, SS.

County of                                                                        , 19      .

Then personally appeared                                                        ,

who acknowledged the foregoing, before me.

_____

Notary Public

My Commission Expires:

# PROPOSAL

From

Proposal No.

Sheet No.

Date

| Proposal Submitted To | Work To Be Performed At |
|---|---|
| Name _____ | Street _____ |
| Street _____ | City _____ State _____ |
| City _____ | Date of Plans _____ |
| State _____ Zip _____ | Architect _____ |
| Telephone Number _____ | |

We hereby propose to furnish all the materials and perform all the labor necessary for the completion of

_____

_____

_____

_____

_____

_____

_____

_____

_____

_____

_____

All material is guaranteed to be as specified, and the above work to be performed in accordance with the drawings and specifications submitted for above work and completed in a substantial workmanlike manner for the sum of _____

_____ Dollars ($ _____ ),

with payments to be made as follows: _____

_____

_____

Any alteration or deviation from above specifications involving extra costs, will be executed only upon written orders, and will become an extra charge over and above the estimate. All agreements are contingent upon strikes, accidents or delays which are beyond our control. Owner to carry fire, tornado and other necessary insurance upon above work. Workmen's Compensation and Public Liability Insurance on above work to be taken out by _____

Respectfully submitted _____

Per _____

NOTE—This proposal may be withdrawn by us if not accepted within _____ days.

## ACCEPTANCE OF PROPOSAL

The above prices, specifications and conditions are satisfactory and are hereby accepted. You are authorized to do the work as specified. Payment will be made as outlined above.

_____

Accepted _____      Signature _____

Date _____      Signature _____

# PRELIEN NOTICE TO OWNER

TO: _____
$\qquad\qquad$ Owner

_____
$\qquad\qquad$ Address

_____

$\qquad$ Please be advised that in accordance with state law, notice is hereby provided that

the undersigned intends to file a mechanic's/materialsman's lien on real property owned

by you and located at

$\qquad$ Such lien is claimed to secure payment of the sum of $ $\qquad$ past

due for labor performed or materials provided by the undersigned within the past

days.

Dated:

_____

_____
$\qquad\qquad$ Address

_____

State of $\qquad\qquad\qquad\qquad\qquad\qquad\qquad\qquad\qquad$ , 19 $\quad$ .

$\qquad\qquad\qquad\qquad$ ,SS.

County of

$\qquad$ Then personally appeared

who acknowledged the foregoing, before me.

_____
Notary Public

My Commission Expires:

# NOTICE OF LIEN
# BY CONTRACTOR

Notice is hereby provided that the below described lienholder provided labor

and/or materials relative to the construction and/or improvements on property known as

_____

Address

_____

City/Town

_____

State, Zip

said real estate more particularly described in Book or Volume                    , Page

, of the                              County Registry of Deeds.

The title owner to said property is:

This lien is filed to secure the balance of $                    , plus statutory

additions due lienholder.

Dated:                                _____

                                      Address

                                      _____

State of

                              ,SS.

County of                                                          , 19        .

Then personally appeared

who acknowledged the foregoing, before me.

_____

Notary Public

My Commission Expires:

# RELEASE OF LIEN

BE IT KNOWN, that _____ (Lienholder), of

_____ , contracted with _____ , on

_____ , 19 _____ , to furnish labor and/or materials for construction at premises

owned by _____ , of _____ ,

which property is described as follows:

On _____ , 19 _____ , lienholder filed for record a notice of lien

against the above described property in the Office of the Registrar of

_____ County, State of _____ , which notice of lien lwas duly recorded in Book

or Volume _____ , Page _____ , of the Lien Records of such County.

In consideration of $ _____ , receipt of which is acknowledged,

lienholder releases the above described property and owner personally from all liability

arising from the labor performed and/or materials furnished by lienholder under the terms

of the above-mentioned contract, and authorizes and directs that the above-mentioned

lien be discharged of record.

Signed under seal this _____ day of _____ , 19 _____ .

_____
Lienholder

State of _____
,SS.
County of _____ , 19 _____ .

Then personally appeared _____ ,

who acknowledged the foregoing, before me.

_____
Notary Public

My Commission Expires:

# LEASES AND TENANCIES

2

# RESIDENTIAL RENTAL APPLICATION

Name of Applicant _____ Telephone _____

Present Address _____

City, State, Zip Code _____

Social Sec. No. _____ Driver's Lic. No. _____

Spouse's Social Sec. No. _____Spouse's Driver's Lic. No. _____

Birth Date _____Spouse's Birth Date _____

How many in your family? Adults _____ Children _____ Any Pets _____

How long have you lived at the present address? _____

Name of Landlord _____ Telephone _____

Employer _____ Position _____

How long? _____ Telephone _____

Salary _____

Spouse's Employer _____ Position _____

How long? _____Telephone _____

Salary _____

Name of Bank _____

_____ Checking _____ Savings      Account No. _____

Additional Personal/Credit References

| Name | Relationship | Telephone |
|---|---|---|
| _____ | _____ | _____ |
| _____ | _____ | _____ |
| _____ | _____ | _____ |

   I represent that the information provided in this application is true to the best of my knowledge. You are hereby authorized to verify my credit and employment references in connection with the processing of this application. I acknowledge receipt of a copy of this application.

Dated: _____ , 19 ___ .      _____
                                 Applicant

# GUARANTY OF RENTS

FOR GOOD CONSIDERATION and as an inducement for

(Landlord) to enter into a lease or tenancy agreement with

(Tenant) for premises at

BE IT KNOWN, that the undersigned does hereby jointly and severally guaranty

to the Landlord and his successors and assigns the prompt, punctual and full payment of

all rents and other charges that may become due and owing from Tenant to Landlord

under said lease or tenancy agreement or any renewal or extension thereof. This

guaranty however shall not extend or apply to any damages incurred by Landlord for any

breach of lease other than the failure to pay rents or other charges due under the lease.

Signed under seal this            day of                        , 19        .

_____
Guarantor

_____
Guarantor

# SUBLEASE

Sublease Agreement entered into between

(Tenant),                                             (Subtenant) and

(Landlord).

Sublease Period: The Subtenant agrees to sublease from Tenant, property

known as

from                              , 19      to                              , 19        .

Terms of Sublease: The Subtenant agrees to comply with all terms and

conditions of the lease entered into by the Tenant, including the prompt payment of all

rents. The lease terms are incorporated into this agreement by reference. The Sub-

tenant agrees to pay the Landlord the monthly rent stated in that lease, and all other

rental charges hereinafter due, and otherwise assume all of Tenant's obligations during

the Sublease period and indemnify Tenant from same.

Security Deposit: The Subtenant agrees to pay to Tenant the sum of $

as a security deposit, to be promptly returned upon the termination of this sublease and

compliance of all conditions.

Inventory: Attached to this agreement is an inventory of items or fixtures on the

above described property on                              , 19      . The Subtenant agrees to

replace or reimburse the Tenant for any of these items that are missing or damaged.

Landlord's Consent: The Landlord consents to this sublease and agrees to

promptly notify the Tenant at                                                             if the

Subtenant is in breach of this agreement. Nothing herein shall constitute a release of

Tenant who shall remain bound under this lease. Nothing herein shall constitute a

consent to any further Sublease or Assignment of Lease.

Date:                                    _____
                                         Landlord


_____        _____
Subtenant                               Tenant

# AMENDMENT TO LEASE

BE IT KNOWN, that for good consideration,

(Landlord) and                                                      (Tenant) under a certain lease

agreement between them for premises known as

_____ , dated _____ , 19 _____ (Lease) hereby

agree to modify and amend said Lease only as to the following terms:

All other Lease terms shall remain in force as contained in the original Lease, which provisions are incorporated herein by reference.

This lease amendment shall become a part of the original Lease and shall be binding upon and inure to the benefit of the parties, their successors, assigns and personal representatives.

Signed under seal this _____ day of _____ , 19 _____

In the presence of:

_____        _____
                                   Landlord


_____        _____
                                   Tenant

# NOTICE TO EXERCISE
# OPTION TO EXTEND LEASE

Date:

TO: _____
Lessor

_____
Address

_____

We hereby refer to a certain lease between us dated

19     , (Lease) for premises described as:

Under the terms of said lease we have the option to extend or renew said lease

for a           year term commencing on         , 19

Pursuant to said lease option provisions, this notice is provided to advise you of

our election to exercise the option to so renew or extend the lease on the terms therein

contained.

_____
Lessee

CERTIFIED MAIL, Return Receipt Requested

# EXTENSION OF LEASE

Agreement to extend lease made by and between

_____ (Landlord) and _____ (Tenant) relative to a

certain lease agreement for premises known as

_____ , said lease dated _____ , 19____ (Lease).

For good consideration, Landlord and Tenant each agree to extend the term of

said Lease for a period of _____ years commencing on _____ , 19____ ,

and terminating on _____ , 19____ , with no further right of renewal or

extension beyond said extended termination date.

During the extended term, Tenant shall pay landlord rent of $ _____

per annum, payable $ _____ per month in advance.  Other modified terms to

lease during the extended term are as follows:

It is further provided, however, that all other terms of the original Lease shall

continue in full force during this extended term, which lease terms are fully incorporated

herein by reference.

This agreement shall be binding upon and shall inure to the benefit of the parties,

their successors, assigns and personal representatives.

Signed under seal this _____ day of _____ , 19____ .

In the presence of:


_____          _____
                                          Landlord


_____          _____
                                          Tenant

# TENANT'S NOTICE
# TO EXERCISE PURCHASE OPTION

Date:

TO:_____
                    Lessor

_____
                    Address

_____

Notice is hereby provided that the undersigned as Lessee under a certain Lease

dated                              , 19      , does hereby exercise its purchase option under

said lease to purchase the property described as

for the option price of $

As contained within the agreement I enclose $                    as a deposit

on said purchase option.

_____
                    Lessee

CERTIFIED MAIL, Return Receipt Requested

# LEASE TERMINATION AGREEMENT

FOR GOOD CONSIDERATION, be it acknowledged, that

(Lessee) and                                        (Lessor) `under

a certain lease agreement between the parties under date of                    , 19

(Lease), do hereby mutually agree to terminate and cancel said Lease effective

, 19        . All rights and obligations under said Lease shall there-

upon be cancelled excepting only for any rents under the Lease accruing prior to the

effective termination date which then remain unpaid or otherwise not satisfied, and which

shall be paid by Lessee on or prior to termination date.

Lessee agrees to promptly surrender the premises to Lessor on or before the

termination date and deliver same to Lessor in good condition free of the Lessee's goods

and effects, waiving all further rights to possession.

This agreement shall be binding upon the parties, their successors, assigns and

personal representatives.


Signed under seal this            day of                    , 19        .

In the presence of:


_____          _____
                                         Lessee


_____          _____
                                         Lessor

# LANDLORD'S NOTICE
# OF ADDITIONAL CHARGES

Date:

TO:_____
                    Tenant

_____
                    Address

_____

You are hereby notified that pursuant to the terms of your lease, the sum of

$                              is due on or before                              , 19      , for

the following described charges:

Payments on the above should be remitted directly to the undersigned.

_____
                                        Landlord

form 23

# NOTICE OF CHANGE
# IN RENT

Date:

TO:_____
Tenant

_____
Address

_____

Please be advised that effective                              , 19      , the monthly

rent for the rented premises you now occupy as my Tenant shall be increased to

$                              per month, payable in advance on the                day of each

month during your continued tenancy.  This is a change from your present rent of

$                              per month.

Very truly,

_____
Landlord

# LANDLORD'S NOTICE TO VACATE

Date:

TO:_____
                    Tenant

_____
                    Address

_____

To the above Tenant and all others now in possession of the below described

premises:

You are hereby notified to vacate the below premises you now occupy

you must deliver possession thereof to the undersigned on or before

19      .

This notice to vacate is due to your following breach of tenancy

If you fail, refuse or neglect to pay your rent, cure the breach, or vacate said

premises within                    days from service of this notice, I will take such legal action as

the law requires to evict you from the premises.  You are to further understand that we

shall in all instances hold you responsible for all present and future rents due under your

tenancy agreement.

_____
                    Landlord

CERTIFIED MAIL, Return Receipt Requested

# LANDLORD'S NOTICE
# TO TERMINATE TENANCY

Date:

TO:_____

Tenant

_____

Address

_____

Please be advised that as your landlord you are hereby notified that we intend to terminate your tenancy on the premises you now occupy as our tenant, said premises described as:

Your tenancy shall be terminated on                              , 19       and we shall require that you deliver to us full possession of the rented premises on said date, free of all your goods and possessions together with all keys to the premises.

Upon your full compliance, and if applicable, we shall thereupon return any security deposit or escrow we may be holding.  Rent for the premises is due and payable through and including the termination date.

_____

Landlord

CERTIFED MAIL, Return Receipt Requested

# TENANT'S NOTICE
# TO TERMINATE TENANCY

Date:

TO:_____
Landlord

_____
Address

_____

Please be advised that as your tenant on certain premises described as:

we hereby notify you of our intention to terminate our tenancy effective

19           . We shall thereupon deliver to you full possession of the premises, together

with the keys, on or before said date and if applicable we request return of any security

deposit or escrow that you may be holding.

_____
Tenant

CERTIFIED MAIL, Return Receipt Requested

# THREE DAY NOTICE TO VACATE
# FOR NON-PAYMENT OF RENT

Date:

TO: _____
         Tenant

_____
         Address

_____

Notice to you and all others in possession, that you are hereby notified to quit and deliver up the premises you hold as our tenant, namely

You are to deliver up said premises on or within three days of receipt of this notice.

This notice is provided due to non-payment of rent.  The present rent arrearage is in the amount of $                         . You may redeem your tenancy by full payment of said arrears within three days as provided under the terms of your tenancy or by state law. In the event you fail to bring your rent payments current or vacate the premises we shall immediately take legal action to evict you and to recover treble rents and damages for the unlawful detention of said premises.

_____
         Landlord

CERTIFIED MAIL, Return Receipt Requested

# LANDLORD'S AND TENANT'S
# MUTUAL RELEASE

BE IT KNOWN, that        (Landlord) hereby

acknowledges that        (Tenant) duly delivered up

possession of the premises known as


and has fully paid all rents due and performed all obligations under said tenancy.

And Tenant acknowledges surrender of said premises as of this date and

acknowledges return of any security deposit due.

Now, therefore, Landlord and Tenant release and discharge one and the other

from any and all claims arising under said tenancy.


Signed under seal this      day of        , 19   .


_____
Landlord


_____
Tenant

# EMPLOYMENT

3

# EMPLOYMENT CONTRACT

EMPLOYMENT CONTRACT between

(Company) and                                          (Employee).

The Company agrees to hire and employ Employee and Employee agrees to be

so employed as a                                          (capacity or job description)

on the following terms:

Employee agrees to faithfully perform the duties assigned to him to the best of

his ability, to devote his full and undivided time to the transaction of Company's business,

to make to Company prompt, complete, and accurate reports of his work and expenses,

to promptly remit to Company all monies of Company collected by him or coming into his

possession and not to engage or be engaged or be interested in any other business

during the existence of this contract, or in any activity in conflict with the interests of the

Company.

In consideration of such service, Company agrees to pay Employee compens-

ation at the rate of

Dollars ($                    ) per                    and his reasonable and necessary

traveling expenses incurred in Company's business while away from the usual place of

business.

Employee shall, when required by Company, reimburse it for the expenses of a

fidelity bond secured by Company and not to exceed

Dollars ($                    ).

This contract shall be in effect from                          , 19      , until it is

terminated by either party at any time on                    days' written notice to the other

party.  At the termination of this agreement in any manner, the payment to Employee of

salary earned to the date of such termination shall be in full satisfaction of all claims against

Company under this agreement.

IN WITNESS WHEREOF, the parties have executed this agreement at

(designate place of execution) on

, 19    .

_____
Company

_____
Employee

# TEMPORARY/PART-TIME EMPLOYMENT
# ACKNOWLEDGEMENT

ACKNOWLEDGEMENT by                                              (Employee).

I understand I am being employed by                            (Company)

in a temporary or part-time position only and for such time as my services are required.  I

understand that this may be temporary and remain part-time and said employment does

not entitle me to any special consideration for permanent or full-time employment.  I

further understand that my temporary or part-time employment may be terminated at any

time without cause or pursuant to disciplinary procedures set forth for permanent or full-

time employees.  I also understand that I am not eligible to participate in any fringe benefit

programs or retirement programs or any other programs available to permanent or  full-time

employees (unless required by law) and in the event I am allowed participation in any

benefit or program, then my continued participation may be voluntarily withdrawn or

terminated by the Company at any time.

_____          _____
                                         Employee

_____          _____
                                         Company

Note: Delete inapplicable words.

# EMPLOYEE NON-COMPETITION AGREEMENT

BE IT KNOWN, for good consideration, and as an inducement for

(Company) to employ

(Employee), the undersigned Employee

hereby unconditionally agrees not to directly or indirectly compete with the business of

the Company and its successors and assigns during the term of employment and for a

period of                years following termination of employment and notwithstanding the

cause or reason for termination or whether the termination was due to the Company.

The term "not to compete" as used herein shall mean that the Employee shall not

own, manage, operate, consult to or be employed in a business substantially similar to or

materially competitive with the present business of the Company or such other business

activity in which the Company may engage during the term of employment.  This agreement

shall extend only to such geographic areas as the Company generally transacts business

within, and shall extend to the existing customers or accounts of the Company no matter

where located.

The Employee acknowledges that the Company shall or may in reliance of this

agreement provide Employee access to trade secrets, customer lists and other con-

fidential and proprietory data and that the provisions of this agreement are reasonably

necessary to protect the Company and its good will.  Upon any breach hereof the

Company shall be entitled to injunctive relief together with money damages at law.

This agreement shall be binding upon and inure to the benefit of the parties, their

successors, assigns and personal representatives.

Signed under seal this            day  of                    , 19      .

In the presence of:


_____          _____
                                         Company


_____          _____
                                         Employee

# EMPLOYEE NON-DISCLOSURE AGREEMENT

BE IT KNOWN, that I,                                                   (Employee)

in consideration of my being employed by

(Company), do hereby agree and acknowledge:

1.      That during the course of my employ there may be disclosed to me certain trade secrets or proprietary information of the Company, said trade secrets consisting of: Technical information; methods, processes, formulae, compositions, systems, techniques, inventions, machines, computer programs, research projects, business information, customer lists, pricing data, sources of supply, financial data and marketing, production, or merchandising systems and plans and other information confidential to the Company.

2.      I further agree that I shall not during, or at any time after the termination of my employment with the Company, and notwithstanding the cause of termination, use for myself or others, or disclose or divulge to others including future employers, any trade secrets, confidential information, or any other proprietary information of the Company in violation of this agreement.

3.      That upon the termination of my employ from the Company: I shall promptly return to the Company all originals and copies of documents and property of the Company, relating in any way to the Company's business, or in any way obtained by me during the course of my employ. I further agree that I shall not retain any copies, notes or abstracts of the foregoing. The Company may notify any future or prospective employer or third party of the existence of this agreement, and shall be entitled to full injunctive relief for any breach. This agreement shall be binding upon me and my personal representatives and successors in interest, and shall inure to the benefit of the Company, its successors and assigns.

Signed under seal this              day of                   , 19    .

_____       _____

Company                                 Employee

# AUTHORIZATION TO RELEASE
# EMPLOYMENT INFORMATION

Date:

TO:_____
           Employer

_____
           Address

_____

The below                                        (Employee) authorizes

the release of the below checked employment information to any third party who makes

request for same.

Those items for which information may be released include:  (Check)

___ Salary

___ Position

___ Department

___ Dates of employment

___ Part-time/full-time or hours worked

___ Garnishes or wage attachments, if any

___ Reason for separation

___ Medical/accident/illness reports

___ Other:

_____
Employee Signature

_____
Address

_____
Date of Employment

_____
Position or Department

# NOTICE OF UNSATISFACTORY PERFORMANCE

Date:

TO:_____
                    Employee

_____
                    Address

_____

Dear

Please accept this as a written confirmation of our meeting reviewing your

performance in your present position.  As it was explained to you, your performance is

unsatisfactory and requires substantial immediate improvement in the following ways:

I sincerely hope that you will make this improvement and become a valued

employee for the company.

Very truly,

_____

cc: File

# FINAL WARNING BEFORE DISMISSAL

Date:

TO:_____
            Employee

_____
            Address

_____

Dear

You have been previously warned of certain problems in your performance as an employee of this company.  These problems include:

There has not been a satisfactory improvement in your performance since your last warning.  Accordingly, any continued violations of company policy or failure to perform according to the standards of our company shall result in immediate termination of your employment without further warning.

Please contact the undersigned or your supervisor if you have any questions.

Very truly,

_____

cc: File

# NOTICE OF DISMISSAL

Date:

TO:_____
Employee

_____
Address

_____

Dear

We regret to inform you that your employment with the firm shall be terminated

effective                                  , 19        , for the following reasons:

Within thirty (30) days of termination we shall issue to you a statement of accrued

benefits.  Severance pay shall be in accordance with company policy.  Any insurance

benefits shall continue in accordance with applicable law and/or the provisions of our

personnel policy.

Please contact                                            at your earliest con-

venience, who will explain each of these items and arrange with you for the return of any

company property.

We sincerely regret this action is necessary, and wish you the best in your future

endeavors.

Very truly,

_____

Copies to:

# RESIGNATION

Date:

TO:_____
                Company

_____
                Address

_____

Gentlemen:

   Please be advised that the undersigned hereby tenders resignation as

_____, effective herewith.  Please acknowledge

receipt and acceptance of this resignation.

   Thank you for your cooperation.

                    Very truly,

                    _____
                    Name

                    _____
                    Address

                    _____

   The foregoing resignation is hereby accepted and is effective as of this

day of _____ , 19      .

                    By_____

# CREDIT AND COLLECTIONS

4

# CONSUMER CREDIT APPLICATION

Name_____Date_____

Address_____ City_____State_____Zip_____

How long at address_____ Own or rent _____

Employed by_____ Position_____

How long_____ Salary   $_____

No. dependents_____Type car owned_____ Year_____

Other sources of income:

_____$_____

_____$_____

Outstanding obligations:

_____$_____

_____$_____

_____$_____

Pending  lawsuits_____

Have you filed bankruptcy within the last 6 years? _____

Credit references:

Name_____Address_____

Name_____Address_____

Name_____Address_____

Bank references:

Name_____ Address  _____

Checking_____ Savings  _____

Visa Card_____ Master Card _____

American Express_____ Other credit cards _____

# NOTICE

When making application for credit, it is understood that an investigation may be made whereby information is obtained through personal interviews with your neighbors, friends, or others with whom you are acquainted.  This inquiry includes information as to your character, general reputation, personal characteristics, and mode of living.  You have a right to make a written request within a reasonable period of time to receive additional, detailed information about the nature and scope of this investigation.

_____

Applicant

# COMMERCIAL CREDIT APPLICATION

Date:_____

Corporate or business name_____

Trade name (if different)_____

Address_____City_____State_____Zip_____

Owner/Manager_____Tel. No._____

How long in business_____D & B Rated_____

Bank References:

Name_____Branch_____Acct. No._____

Name_____Branch_____Acct. No._____

Trade References:

Name_____Address_____

Name_____Address_____

Name_____Address_____

Credit line requested $_____

Pending lawsuits against company:_____

_____

_____

Are financial statements available? _____

The undersigned authorizes inquiry as to credit information. We further acknowledge that credit privileges, if granted, may be withdrawn at any time and certify the above information to be true.

_____

# REQUEST FOR CREDIT REFERENCE

Date:

TO:_____

_____
Address

_____

Gentlemen:

Re:

Please be advised the above captioned party has recently applied for credit and

listed you as a credit reference.  So that we may have proper information on which to make

our credit decision, would you advise us of your credit experience with this party by

providing us the following information:

High credit limit:

Low credit limit:

Terms of sale:

How long sold:

Present balance owed:

Payment history:

Please note other credit information you may believe useful on the reverse side.

This information shall, of course, be held strictly confidential.

A stamped return envelope is enclosed for your convenience.

Very truly,

_____

_____
Address

_____

# AUTHORIZATION TO RELEASE
# CREDIT INFORMATION

Date:

TO:_____
Creditor

_____
Address

_____

Please be advised I have a credit account with your firm and hereby request that a

report of my credit history with you be forwarded to the below listed credit reporting

agencies, and you may consider this letter as my authorization to release this information.

Thank you for your cooperation.

_____
Signature

_____
Address

_____
Signature of Joint Applicant (if any)

_____
Name of Account

_____
Account Number

Credit Reporting Agencies:

_____      _____
Agency                                Address

_____      _____

_____      _____

_____      _____

# NOTICE ON CREDIT REQUEST

Date:

TO: _____

_____
Address

_____

Gentlemen:

Thank you for your recent order dated _____ , 19 _____ , however we

cannot release this order on credit terms for the reasons checked:

_____ Credit information incomplete

_____ Insufficient credit references

_____ Unacceptable credit references

_____ Unable to verify credit data

_____ Income insufficient

_____ Temporary or irregular employment

_____ Inadequate term of residence

_____ Limited credit experience

_____ Poor credit performance with us

_____ Adverse credit reports

_____ Collection actions against you

_____ Outstanding liens or judgements

_____ Bankruptcy

_____ Other:

Comments:

We hope you understand the reason for this decision.

Very truly,

_____

# REQUEST FOR DISCLOSURE
# OF CREDIT INFORMATION

Date:

TO:_____

Credit Reporting Agency

_____

Address

_____

In accordance with the Federal Fair Credit Reporting Act, I hereby request a full

and complete disclosure of my credit file.  This should include both the sources of

information on my file and the names and addresses of any party who has received my

credit report whether in writing, orally or by other electronic means.

Thank you for your cooperation.

| | |
|---|---|
| Signature | Printed Full Name |
| | |
| Social Security Number | Address |
| | |
| Telephone Number | Prior or Other Names |
| | |
| | Prior or Other Addresses |

State of

,SS.

County of                                                                                    , 19    .

Then personally appeared

who acknowledged the foregoing, before me.

_____

Notary Public

My Commission Expires:

# ADVERSE CREDIT
# INFORMATION REQUEST

Date:

TO:_____

            Creditor

_____

            Address

_____

     I have recently been declined credit by your firm on the transaction described below. In accordance with the Federal Fair Credit Reporting Act, I am requesting a full and complete disclosure of the reasons for this denial of credit and the nature of any adverse credit information received from any source other than a consumer reporting agency, including the identity of such source that submitted adverse credit information against me.

_____     _____
Signed                              Full Name

_____     _____
Date of Credit Application          Address

_____     _____
Transaction or Type Credit          Telephone Number

State of

                         , SS.

County of                                            , 19   .

     Then personally appeared

who acknowledged the foregoing, before me.

_____
Notary Public

My Commission Expires:

# NOTICE TO CORRECT
# CREDIT INFORMATION

Date:

TO _____
          Credit Reporting Agency

_____
          Address

_____

Gentlemen:

A review of my credit file discloses the following adverse credit report:

This information is erroneous or incomplete in the following respects:  (Use reverse side for additional space.)

In accordance with the provisions of the Fair Credit Reporting Act, I request that this letter be made part of my credit file and thereupon disseminated with any credit request on me.

Very truly,

_____

_____
          Address

_____

# PAYMENT ON SPECIFIC ACCOUNTS

Date:

TO:_____
                    Creditor

_____
                    Address

_____

Gentlemen:

   We enclose our check no.              in the amount of $              as payment

for and to be credited to the following charges or invoices only:


            Account/Invoice/Debt                    Amount

   _____        $_____

   _____        $_____

   _____        $_____

   _____        $_____

   _____        $_____

                        Total                $_____


   Please be certain that payment herein is applied only to the specific items listed

and not applied, in whole or in part, to any other outstanding obligation.


                    Very truly,



            _____

# NOTICE OF DISPUTED
# ACCOUNT BALANCE

Date:

To: _____
          Creditor/Supplier

_____
          Address

_____

Gentlemen:

We refer to your invoice or statement no.                              , dated

              , 19          in the amount of $

We dispute the balance claimed for the following reason(s):

_____ Items billed for have not been received.

_____ Prices are in excess of agreed amount.  Credit of $                    claimed.

_____ Prior payment made in the amount of $                    on                    ,

          19          was not credited.

_____ Goods were unordered, and are available for return on shipping

          instructions.

_____ Goods were defective as per prior notice.

_____ Goods are available for return and credit per sales terms.

_____ Other:

Therefore, we request you credit our account in the amount of $

See reverse side for any additional information or explanation.

                    Very truly,


                    _____
                    Title

                    _____
                    Account

                    _____
                    Address

# REQUEST FOR INFORMATION
# ON DISPUTED CHARGE

Date: _____

TO: _____
                    Supplier

_____
                    Address

_____

Gentlemen:

Please be advised that we have received your statement of charges and we dispute certain charges on our account for the following stated reasons:



We do want to reconcile our account, so we may pay and resolve this matter, however, we find we need the below checked information or documents:

____ Copies of charges noted on reverse side

____ Copies of purchase orders

____ Debit memoranda outstanding

____ List of goods claimed as shipped

____ Other:



Thank you for your immediate attention and upon receipt we shall give your statement our prompt consideration.

Very truly,


_____

# SETTLEMENT ON DISPUTED ACCOUNT

Agreement by and between                                                          (Creditor)

and                                                    (Debtor).

Whereas,                                                    (Creditor) asserts to

hold a certain claim against                                                    (Debtor) in

the amount of $                                   arising from the below described transaction:



And whereas, Debtor disputes said claim, and denies said debt is due,

And whereas, the parties desire to resolve and forever settle and adjust said

claim.

Now, therefore, Debtor agrees to pay to Creditor and Creditor agrees to accept

from Debtor simultaneous herewith, the sum of $                                 in full payment,

settlement, satisfaction, discharge and release of said claim and in release of any further

claims thereto.

This agreement shall be binding upon and inure to the benefit of the parties, their

successors, assigns and personal representatives.

Signed under seal this                          day of                                  , 19          .


Witnesseth:


_____          _____
                                                          Creditor


_____          _____
                                                          Debtor

# AGREEMENT TO COMPROMISE DEBT

BE IT KNOWN, for good consideration, the undersigned as a creditor of

(Debtor) hereby enters into this agreement to

compromise and discharge the indebtedness due from Debtor to the undersigned on the

following terms and conditions:

1.      The Debtor and the undersigned acknowledge that the present debt due and

owing creditor is in the amount of $

2.      The parties agree that the undersigned creditor shall accept the sum of $

as full and total payment on said debt and in complete discharge, release, satisfaction and

settlement of all monies presently due, provided the sum herein shall be fully and punc-

tually  paid in the manner following:



3.      In the event the Debtor fails to fully and  punctually pay the compromised amount,

the undersigned creditor shall have full rights to prosecute its claim for the full amount of

$                          less credits for payments made.

4.      In the event of default in payment the Debtor agrees to pay all reasonable

attorneys' fees and costs of collection.

5.      This agreement shall be binding upon and inure to the benefit of the parties, their

successors, assigns and personal representatives.

Signed under seal this              day of                          , 19          .

Witnesseth:

_____     _____
                                    Creditor


_____     _____
                                    Debtor

# NOTICE OF DEFAULT
# ON PROMISSORY NOTE

Date:

TO:_____
  Borrower

_____
  Address

_____

We refer to your promissory note dated _____ , 19____ , in

the original principal amount of $_____ and to which we, the under-

signed, are holder.

Notice is hereby provided that you are in default under said note in that the

following payment(s) have not been received.

<u>Payment Due Date</u>                                        <u>Amount Due</u>

_____

Total Arrears          $

Accordingly, demand is hereby made for full payment of the entire balance of

$_____ due under the note.  If payment is not received within

_____ days, this note shall be forwarded to our attorneys for collection and you shall additionally

be liable for all reasonable costs of collection.

Very truly,

_____

# DEMAND TO ENDORSERS FOR PAYMENT

Date:

TO:_____

Endorser

_____

Address

_____

Please be advised that the undersigned is the holder of the below described (check) (note) to which you are an endorser:

Maker:

Date:

Face Amount:

Notice is hereby provided that said instrument has been dishonored and has not been paid, and protest and demand is hereby made upon you to immediately pay the amount due in the amount of $

In the event payment is not made within five (5) days, the undersigned shall commence to suit on your warranties of endorsement.

Upon full payment on your endorsement, we shall assign to you all our rights, title and interest as we have to the instrument.

Very truly,

_____

CERTIFIED MAIL, Return Receipt Requested

# DEMAND ON CO-TENANT
# FOR PAYMENT

Date:

TO:_____

_____
Address

_____

Please be advised that the undersigned is owed $                    for the

following:

This debt was incurred in respect to the above property in which you are a tenant

in common.

Demand is hereby made upon you for payment of $                    repre-

senting your pro rata share of the obligation.

_____

_____
Address

_____

# DEMAND TO GUARANTORS FOR PAYMENT

Date:

TO: _____
Guarantor

_____
Address

_____

Please be advised that the undersigned is the holder of your guaranty dated

, 19 , wherein you guarantee the debt owed us by

, as Obligor.

Please be advised that payments on said debt are in default. Accordingly,

demand is made upon you as a guarantor for full payment on the outstanding debt

now due in the amount of $

In the event payment on your guaranty is not made within days

from date above, we shall proceed to enforce our rights against you under the

guaranty and shall additionally hold you responsible for attorneys' fees and costs of

collection as provided for under your guaranty.

Very truly,

_____

CERTIFIED MAIL, Return Receipt Requested

# FINAL NOTICE BEFORE
# LEGAL ACTION

Date:

TO:_____

_____
Address

_____

Gentlemen:

We have repeatedly notified you of your long overdue balance in the amount of

$

Since you have ignored our requests for payment we have turned your account

over to our attorneys and instructed them to commence suit against you without further

delay.

There is still time, however, to avoid suit if you contact us within the next five (5)

days, and make satisfactory arrangements for payment.

This will be your final opportunity to resolve matters without the expense or

inconvenience of court proceedings.

Very truly,

_____

# OVERDUE ACCOUNT
# COLLECTION TRANSMITTAL

Date:

TO:_____

Attorney/Collection Agency

_____

Address

_____

Gentlemen:

We are turning over to you the following accounts for collection in accordance with your standard fee schedule.

We would appreciate an expedited effort to collect said accounts. We also enclose our files, supporting invoices or documents.

Please call if you need further information.

Very truly,

_____

_____

Address

_____

Account                                    Balance Owed

_____          _____

_____          _____

_____          _____

_____          _____

_____          _____

# RECEIPT IN FULL

The Undersigned hereby acknowledges receipt of the sum of $                    ,

from                                                          , this date by

cash _____ check _____; said payment to be applied and credited to the below

described account; and accepted as full payment and satisfaction of all monies due.

Date:

_____

# RECEIPT ON ACCOUNT

The Undersigned hereby acknowledges receipt of the sum of $                    ,

from                                                            , this date by

cash _____check _____; said payment to be applied as partial payment on account.

Date:


_____

# CHECK STOP-PAYMENT ORDER

Date:

TO:_____
                    Bank

_____
                  Address

_____

Gentlemen:

Please be advised that you are hereby directed to place a stop-payment order

and refuse payment against our account upon presentment of the following check:

Name of Payee:

Date of Check:

Check Number:

Amount:

This stop payment order shall remain in effect until further written notice.

Please advise if this check has been previously paid, and the date of payment.

_____
Name of Account

_____
Account Number

By: _____

This form should be reissued after six months.

# NOTICE OF DISHONORED CHECK

Date:

TO:_____

_____
Address

_____

Please take notice that payment on your check no.            in the amount of

$                  , tendered to us on                  , 19        has been

refused by your bank because of insufficient funds. We have verified with your bank that

there are still insufficient funds to pay the check.

Accordingly, we demand that you replace this check with a cash (or certified

check) payment.

Unless we receive good funds for said amount within            days, or such

further time as may be allowed pursuant to state law, we shall immediately commence

appropriate legal action to protect our interests.  Upon receipt of good replacement funds

we shall return to you the dishonored check.

Very truly,

_____

CERTIFIED MAIL, Return Receipt Requested

# DISHONORED CHECK PLACED
# FOR BANK COLLECTION

Date:

TO:_____
    Depository Bank

    _____
            Address

    _____

Gentlemen:

   We enclose and place with you for collection and credit to our account the below described check previously returned to us due to insufficient/uncollected funds:

        Maker:

        Date of Check:

        Amount:

        Drawee Bank:

        Check Number:

        Account Number:

   Please charge our account the customary service fee for handling this check on a collection basis.

   We would appreciate your notifying us when the check clears, or alternatively please return the check to us should the check remain unpaid beyond the collection period.

        Very truly,

        _____
        Signatory

        _____
        Name of Account

        _____
        Account Number

# NOTICE OF LOST CREDIT CARD

Date:

TO:_____

_____
Address

_____

Gentlemen:

Please be advised that the below described credit card has been lost and you are therefore requested to stop issuance of further credit against said card until notified to the contrary.

Please notify me at once if charges appeared against said card after date of

_____ , 19_____ , as this was the date card was lost and therefore subsequent charges were unauthorized.

Thank you for your cooperation.

Very truly,

_____
Cardholder

_____
Address

_____
Credit Card Number

CERTIFIED MAIL, Return Receipt Requested

# NOTICE TO DECLINE
# CREDIT ISSUANCE

Date:

TO: _____
Credit Card Company

_____
Address

_____

Gentlemen:

Please be advised that on                    , 19        the undersigned charged the

sum of $                         on a transaction with

(Company).

We hereby instruct you not to honor said charge or issue payment to the company for

the following reason:

Thank you for your cooperation.

_____
Cardholder

_____
Address

_____
Credit Card Number

CERTIFIED MAIL, Return Receipt Requested

# NOTICE OF RESCISSION

Date:

TO:_____

_____
Address

_____

Gentlemen:

　　We have entered into a transaction with you on _____ , 19 ,

described as follows:

　　We hereby notify you of our rescission of said contract which rescission is made

within three (3) days from the contract date.

　　Pursuant to the Federal Truth in Lending Act, we hereby request the return of our

deposit in the amount of $ _____ and the cancellation of any lien against

our property and request same within ten (10) days as required by law.

Very truly,

_____
Name

_____
Address

_____

# LOANS AND DEBTS

**5**

# INSTALLMENT NOTE

FOR VALUE RECEIVED, the undersigned promise to pay to the order of

the sum of

($               ) Dollars, together with annual interest of        % on any unpaid balance.
Principal with interest, shall be paid in            installments of $
each, with a first payment due                  , 19     , and the same amount on the
same day of each            thereafter until the entire principal amount of this note and
earned interest is fully paid.  All payments shall be first applied to earned interest and the
balance to principal.  The undersigned may prepay this note in whole or in part without
penalty.

This note shall be fully payable upon demand of any holder in the event the
undersigned shall default in making any payments due under this note within            days
of its due date, or upon the death, bankruptcy or insolvency of any of the undersigned.

In the event of any default, the undersigned agree to pay all reasonable attorneys'
fees and costs of collection to the extent permitted by law.  This note shall take effect as a
sealed instrument and be enforced in accordance with the laws of the payee's state.  All
parties to this note waive presentment, demand, protest, and all notices thereto, and agree
to remain fully bound notwithstanding any extension, indulgence, modification or release or
discharge of any party or collateral under this note.  The undersigned shall be jointly and
severally liable under this note.

Signed under seal this            day of                  , 19     .

In the presence of:

_____          _____
                                          Maker

_____          _____
                                          Maker

# DEMAND PROMISSORY NOTE

FOR VALUE RECEIVED, the undersigned promise to pay to the order of

, the sum of

($                    ) Dollars, with annual interest at           % on the unpaid balance.

The full unpaid principal and any earned interest shall be fully due and immediately payable

UPON DEMAND of any holder of this note.

Upon failure to make payment within            days of demand, and should this

note be turned over for collection, the undersigned shall pay all reasonable legal fees and

costs of collection.  All parties to this note waive presentment, demand, notice of non-

payment, protest and notice of protest, and agree to remain fully bound notwithstanding

the release of any party or extension, indulgence, modification of terms, or discharge of any

collateral for this note.  The undersigned shall be jointly and severally liable under this note.

Signed under seal this            day of                    , 19      .

In the presence of:

_____        _____
                                        Maker

_____        _____
                                        Maker

# BALLOON NOTE

FOR VALUE RECEIVED, the undersigned promise to pay to the order of

, the sum of

($                    ) Dollars, with annual

interest of        % on any unpaid balance.

This note shall be paid in                consecutive and equal installments of

$                each with a first payment one            from date hereof, and the

same amount on the same day of each              thereafter, provided the entire

principal balance and any accrued but unpaid interest shall be fully paid on or before

, 19        . This note may be prepaid without penalty. All payments

shall be first applied to earned interest and the balance to principal.

This note shall be due and payable upon demand of any holder hereof should

any payment due hereunder not be made within          days of its due date. All

parties to this note waive presentment, demand and protest, and all notices thereto. In

the event of default, the undersigned agree to pay all costs of collection and reasonable

attorneys' fees to the extent permitted by law. The undersigned shall be jointly and

severally liable under this note.

Signed under seal this            day of                , 19      .

In the presence of:

_____     _____
                                    Maker


_____     _____
                                    Maker

# TIME NOTE

FOR VALUE RECEIVED, the undersigned promise to pay  to the order of

, the sum of

($                    ) Dollars, payable with annual interest of              % on any

unpaid balance.

All principal and earned interest shall be fully due and payable on

19          , time being of the essence.

The maker may prepay this note, in whole or in part, without penalty.

All parties to this note waive presentment, demand, protest or notices thereto

and agree to remain bound notwithstanding any indulgence, modification or release or

discharge of any party or collateral securing this note.  The undersigned shall be jointly

and severally liable under this note.

Upon default, the undersigned agree to pay all reasonable attorneys' fees and

costs of collection to the extent permitted by law.


Signed under seal this              day of                          , 19        .


In the presence of:


_____        _____
                                        Maker


_____        _____
                                        Maker

# UNLIMITED GUARANTY

FOR VALUE RECEIVED, and as an inducement for

(Creditor) to extend credit time to time to

(Borrower), the undersigned jointly and severally and unconditionally guarantee to

Creditor the prompt and full payment of all sums now or hereinafter due Creditor from

Borrower.

The undersigned agree to remain fully bound on this guaranty notwithstanding

any extension, forebearance, modification, waiver, or release, discharge or substitution of

any party, collateral or security for the debt, and the undersigned consent to and waive all

notice of same. In the event of default, the Creditor may seek payment directly from the

undersigned without need to proceed first against the Borrower. The undersigned waive

all suretyship defenses generally.

The undersigned further agree to pay all reasonable attorneys' fees and costs

necessary for the enforcement of this guaranty.

This guaranty is unlimited as to amount or duration provided that any guarantor

hereto may terminate his obligations as to future credit extended after delivery of notice of

guaranty termination to the Creditor by certified mail, return receipt, and provided that said

termination notice shall not discharge guarantor's obligations as to debts incurred to date

of termination.

This guaranty shall be binding upon and inure to the benefit of the parties, their

successors, assigns and personal representatives.

Signed under seal this               day of                               , 19            .

In the presence of:

_____          _____
                                          Guarantor


_____          _____
                                          Guarantor

# LIMITED GUARANTY

BE IT KNOWN, for good consideration, and as an inducement for

(Creditor) to extend credit from time to time to

(Customer) the undersigned jointly, severally

and unconditionally guarantee to Creditor the prompt and punctual payment of certain

sums now or hereinafter due Creditor from Customer, provided that the liability of the

guarantors hereunder, whether singularly or collectively, shall be limited to the sum of

$ as a maximum liability and guarantors shall not be liable under this

guarantee for any greater or further amount.

The undersigned guarantors agree to remain fully bound on this guarantee,

notwithstanding any extension, forebearance, indulgence or waiver, or release or dis-

charge or substitution of any party or collateral or security for the debt. In the event of

default, Creditor may seek payment directly from the undersigned without need to pro-

ceed first against borrower. Guarantors further waive all suretyship defenses consistent

with this limited guaranty.

In the event of default, the guarantor shall be responsible for all attorneys' fees

and reasonable costs of collection, which may be in addition to the limited guaranty

amount.

This guaranty shall be binding upon and inure to the benefit of the parties, their

successors, assigns and personal representatives.

Signed under seal this             day of                           , 19        .

In the presence of:


_____         _____
                                             Guarantor


_____         _____
                                             Guarantor

# SPECIFIC GUARANTY

FOR GOOD AND VALUABLE CONSIDERATION and as an inducement for

(Creditor) to extend credit to

(Borrower), the undersigned jointly,

severally and unconditionally guarantee to Creditor the prompt and full payment of the

following specific debt owed to Creditor from Borrower:


And the undersigned agree to remain bound on this guaranty notwithstanding

any extension, renewal, indulgence, forebearance or waiver, or release, discharge or

substitution of any collateral or security for the debt.  In the event of default, the Creditor

may seek payment directly from the undersigned without need to proceed first against

Borrower, and the undersigned waive all suretyship defenses.

The obligations of the undersigned under this guarantee shall be only to the

specific debt described and to no other debt or obligation between Borrower and

Creditor.

In the event of default, the guarantor shall be responsible for all attorneys' fees

and reasonable costs of collection.

This guaranty shall be binding upon and inure to the benefit of the parties, their

successors, assigns and personal representatives.

Signed under seal this             day of                         , 19       .

In the presence of:


_____          _____
                                          Guarantor


_____          _____
                                          Guarantor

# GUARANTY REVOCATION

Date:

TO: _____
_____Creditor_____

_____
_____Address_____

_____

We refer to our guaranty dated _____ , 19____ , wherein we guaranteed the credit of _____ (Obligor).

Effective upon receipt of this letter (or such effective termination date as provided under the guaranty) we shall not be obligated under the guaranty for any future credit extended by you to the Obligor, as we thereupon revoke our guaranty. We understand that we shall remain liable for the present balance owed until fully paid.

Please confirm the present balance owed and please notify when said balance has been fully paid, together with return of our guaranty at that time.

Please confirm below receipt and acknowledgement of this guaranty revocation by return acknowledgement below.

Sincerely,

_____
Guarantor

_____
Guarantor

CERTIFIED MAIL, Return Receipt Requested

Acknowledged:

_____
Creditor

Effective Date:_____     Present Balance: $_____

# SECURITY AGREEMENT

Date:

BE IT KNOWN, that for good consideration

of                                                                      (Debtor) grants to

of

and its successors and assigns (Secured Party) a security interest pursuant to Article 9 of

the Uniform Commercial Code in the following property (collateral), which shall include all

after acquired property of a like nature and description and proceeds and products

thereof:

This security interest is granted to secure payment and performance on the

following obligations now or hereinafter owed Secured Party from Debtor:

Debtor hereby acknowledges to Secured Party that:

1.      The collateral shall be kept at the Debtor's above address and not moved or

relocated without written consent.

2.      The Debtor warrants that it owns the collateral and it is free from any other lien,

encumbrance and security interest or adverse interest and the Debtor has full authority to

grant this security interest.

3.      Debtor agrees to execute such financing statements as are reasonably required

by Secured Party to perfect this security agreement in accordance with state law and the

Uniform Commercial Code.

4.      Upon default in payment or performance of any obligation for which this security interest is granted, or breach of any term of this security agreement, then in such instance Secured Party may declare all obligations immediately due and payable and shall have all remedies of a secured party under the Uniform Commercial Code, as enacted in the Debtor's state, which rights shall be cumulative and not necessarily successive with any other rights or remedies.

5.      Debtor agrees to maintain such insurance coverage on the collateral as Secured Party may from time to time reasonably require and Secured Party shall be named as loss payee.

6.      This security agreement shall further be in default upon the death, insolvency or bankruptcy of any party who is an obligor to this agreement or upon any material decrease in the value of the collateral or adverse change in the financial condition of the Debtor.

7.      Upon default the Debtor shall pay all reasonable attorneys' fees and costs of collection necessary to enforce this agreement.

IN WITNESS WHEREOF, this agreement is signed under seal this          day of

_____ , 19    .

_____
Debtor

_____
Secured Party

Note:   Record this security agreement or financing statements in appropriate filing office to protect your rights against third parties.

# PLEDGE OF PERSONAL PROPERTY

BE IT KNOWN, for value received, the undersigned (Pledgor) hereby deposits, delivers to and pledges with

(Pledgee) as collateral security to secure the payment of the following described debt owing Pledgee:

The collateral consisting of the following personal property (collateral):

It is further agreed that:

1.     Pledgee may assign or transfer said debt and the pledged collateral hereunder to any third party.

2.     Pledgee shall have no liability for loss, destruction or casualty to the collateral unless caused by its own negligence, or the negligence of any assignee.

3.     The Pledgor shall pay any and all insurance it elects to maintain, or the Pledgee reasonably requires on the pledged collateral and shall pay any personal property, excise or other tax or levy.

4.     The Pledgor warrants that it has good title to the pledged collateral, full authority to pledge same and that said collateral is free of any adverse lien, encumbrance or adverse claim.

5.     Upon default of payment of the debt or breach of this pledge agreement, the Pledgee or holder shall have full rights to foreclose on the pledged collateral and exercise its rights as a secured party pursuant to Article 9 of the Uniform Commercial

Code; said rights being cumulative with any other rights the Pledgee or holder may have against the Pledgor.

Pledgor understands that upon foreclosure the pledged property may be sold at public auction or private sale. The Pledgor shall be provided reasonable notice of any said intended public or private sale and the Pledgor shall have full rights to redeem said collateral at any time prior to said sale upon payment of the balance due hereunder together with accrued fees and expenses of collection. In the event the collateral shall be sold for less than the amount then owing, the Pledgor shall be liable for any deficiency.

Upon payment of the obligation for which the collateral is pledged, the property shall be returned to the Pledgor and this pledge agreement shall be terminated.

This pledge agreement shall be binding upon and inure to the benefit of the parties, their successors, assigns and personal representatives.

Upon default the Pledgor shall pay all reasonable attorneys' fees and costs of collection.

Signed under seal this _____ day of _____ , 19 ___ .

In the presence of:

_____     _____
                                      Pledgor

_____     _____
                                      Pledgee

# PLEDGE OF SHARES OF STOCK

BE IT KNOWN, for value received, the undersigned (Pledgor) hereby
deposits. delivers to, and pledges with

(Pledgee) as collateral security to secure the payment of the following described debt
owing Pledgee:

The shares of stock, described as                    shares of stock of

(Corporation) represented as stock certificate no(s).

It is further agreed that:

1.      Pledgee may assign or transfer said debt and the collateral pledged hereunder to any third party.

2.      In the event a stock dividend or further issue of stock in the Corporation is
issued to the Pledgor, the Pledgor shall pledge said shares as additional collateral for
the debt.

3.      That during the term of this pledge agreement, and so long as it is not in
default, the Pledgor shall have full rights to vote said shares and shall be entitled to all
dividend income, except that stock dividends shall also be pledged.

4.      That during the term of this agreement, the Pledgor shall not issue any proxy
or assignment of rights to the pledged shares.

5.      The Pledgor warrants and represents it has good title to the shares being
pledged, they are free from liens and encumbrances or prior pledge, and the Pledgor
has full authority to transfer said shares as collateral security.

6.      Upon default of payment of the debt, or breach of this pledge agreement, the
Pledgee or holder shall have full rights to foreclose on the pledged shares and

exercise its rights as a secured party pursuant to Article 9 of the Uniform Commercial Code, said rights being cumulative with any other rights the Pledgee or holder may have against the Pledgor.

Pledgor understands that upon foreclosure the pledged shares may be sold at public auction or private sale. The Pledgor shall be provided reasonable notice of said intended public or private sale and the Pledgor shall have full rights to redeem said shares at any time prior to said sale upon payment of the balance due hereunder, and accrued costs of collection. In the event the shares shall be sold for less than the amount then owing, the Pledgor shall be liable for any deficiency.

Upon payment of the obligation for which the shares are pledged, the shares shall be returned to the Pledgor and this pledge agreement shall be terminated.

This pledge agreement shall be binding upon and inure to the benefit of the parties, their successors, assigns and personal representatives.

Upon default the Pledgor shall pay all reasonable attorneys' fees and costs of collection.

Signed under seal this                 day of                           , 19

In the presence of:


_____        _____
                                        Pledgor


_____        _____
                                        Pledgee

# SUBORDINATION AGREEMENT

BE IT KNOWN, for value received, the Undersigned hereby subordinates any and all claims or other rights to monies due as now or hereinafter owed the Undersigned from _____ (Debtor) to any and all claims as may now or hereinafter be due _____ (Creditor) from said Debtor and notwithstanding whether said Debtor is primarily or secondarily liable on said debt, and notwithstanding the date the respective debts were incurred.

The subordination herein shall be unconditional, irrevocable and unlimited both as to amount or duration and notwithstanding whether the respective claims against Debtor are now or hereinafter secured or unsecured in whole or in part, and notwithstanding such other rights to priority as may exist, and the undersigned shall forebear on collecting any monies due on its claim until all claims due Creditor from Debtor have been fully paid.

This agreement shall be binding upon and inure to the benefit of the parties, their successors, assigns and personal representatives.

Signed under seal this _____ day of _____, 19____ .

Witnesseth:

_____        _____

_____        _____
                                        Creditor

Assented to:


_____
Debtor

# AGREEMENT TO ASSUME OBLIGATION

BE IT KNOWN, for good consideration, this Agreement is entered into between

(Creditor) and

(Customer) and                                                    (Undersigned).

It is hereby acknowledged and agreed that:

1.      Both the Customer and Creditor confirm that Customer presently owes Creditor

the sum of $                                    (Debt), which sum is fully due and payable.

2.      The undersigned unconditionally and irrevocably agrees to assume and fully pay

said Debt and otherwise guarantee to both Creditor and Customer the prompt payment of

said debt on the terms below, and to fully indemnify and save harmless Creditor and

Customer from any loss thereto.

3.      Said Debt shall be promptly paid in the manner following:

4.      This shall not constitute a release or discharge of the obligations of Customer to

Creditor for the payment of said Debt, provided that so long as the undersigned shall

promptly pay the Debt in the manner above described, Creditor shall forebear in

commencing collection action against Customer.  In the event of default of payment,

Creditor shall have full rights, jointly and severally, against both Customer and/or

undersigned for any balance then owing.  This Agreement extends only to the above

debt and to no other or greater obligation.

5.      This agreement shall be binding upon and inure to the benefit of the parties, their

successors, assigns and personal representatives.

Signed under seal this                     day of                              , 19       .

In the presence of:

_____        _____

_____        _____
                                        Creditor

_____        _____
                                        Customer

# SALE OF
# PERSONAL PROPERTY

6

# AGREEMENT FOR PURCHASE
# OF PERSONAL PROPERTY

Purchase and Sales Agreement made by and between

(Seller) and                                                            (Buyer).

Whereas, for good consideration the parties mutually agree that:

1.      Seller agrees to sell, and Buyer agrees to buy the following described property:



2.      Buyer agrees to pay to Seller and Seller agrees to accept the total purchase price

of $                              , payable as follows:

      $                                        deposit herewith paid

      $                                        payable on delivery by cash, or certified check

3.      Seller warrants it has good and legal title to said property, full authority to sell said

property, and that said property shall be sold by warranty bill of sale free and clear of all

liens, encumbrances, liabilities and adverse claims of every nature and description.

4.      Said property is sold in "as is" condition, Seller disclaiming any warranty of

merchantability, fitness or working order or condition of the property except that it shall be

sold in its present condition, reasonable wear and tear excepted.

5.      The parties agree to transfer title on                                     , 19        , at

the address of the Seller.

6.      This agreement shall be binding upon and inure to the benefit of the parties, their

successors, assigns and personal representatives.

      Signed under seal this                  day of                       , 19        .

Witnesseth:

_____          _____
                                     Seller

_____          _____
                                       Buyer

# CONDITIONAL SALES CONTRACT

CONDITIONAL SALES AGREEMENT between

(Seller) and                                          (Buyer) wherein the Seller

agrees to sell to Buyer the following goods on a conditional sale:

| | |
|---|---|
| Sales price | $_____ |
| Sales tax (if any) | $_____ |
| Finance charge (if any) | $_____ |
| Insurance (if any) | $_____ |
| Other charges (if any) | $_____ |
| Total purchase price | $_____ |

Less:

| | |
|---|---|
| Down payment | $_____ |
| Other credits | $_____ |

| | |
|---|---|
| Total credits | $_____ |
| Amount financed | $_____ |

ANNUAL INTEREST RATE          _____%

The above amount financed shall be payable in          (weekly/monthly)

installments of $          each, commencing one (week/month) from date hereof

and continuing until fully paid.

Seller shall retain title to goods until payment of the full purchase price, subject to

allocation of payments and release of security interest as required by law.  The under-

signed agrees to safely keep the goods free from other liens and encumbrances at the

below address, and not remove goods without consent of Seller.  Buyer agrees to execute all financing statements as may be required of Seller to perfect this conditional sales agreement.

The entire balance shall become immediately due upon default upon the payment of any installment due or other breach of this agreement.

Upon default, Seller may enter upon premises of Buyer and reclaim said goods. Upon retaking said goods, the Seller shall have the right to resell same for credit to the balance purchased, and Seller may itself reacquire same all as further defined and set forth under applicable state.

At the election of Seller, the Buyer shall keep goods adequately insured, naming Seller loss payee, and providing Seller evidence of insurance.

The full balance shall become due on default with the undersigned paying all reasonable attorneys' fees and costs of collection. Upon default, Seller shall have the further right to retake the goods, hold and dispose of same and collect expenses, together with any deficiency due from Buyer, but subject to the Buyer's right to redeem pursuant to law and the Uniform Commercial Code.

THIS IS A CONDITIONAL SALE AGREEMENT.

Signed under seal this _____ day of _____ , 19 _____ .

Accepted:

_____     _____
Seller                                Buyer

_____     _____
Address                               Address

By_____     By_____

Note:  Record this Agreement or Financing Statements as required by state law to
        protect your rights.

# CONSIGNMENT AGREEMENT

Agreement made this            day of                            , 19      , by and

between                                                      (Consignor) and

(Customer).

1.      Customer acknowledges receipt of goods as described on annexed schedule. Said goods shall remain property of Consignor until sold.  Consignor may from time to time ship additional consigned goods as ordered.

2.      The Customer at its own cost and expense agrees to keep and display the goods only in its place of business, and agrees, on demand made before any sale, to return the same in good order and condition.  Customer may at its own election return goods to Consignor.

3.      The Customer agrees to use its best efforts to sell the goods for the Consignor's account on cash terms, and at such prices as shall from time to time be set by Consignor, and at no lesser price.

4.      The Customer agrees, upon sale, to maintain proceeds due Consignor in trust, and separate and apart from its own funds and deliver such proceeds, less commission, to Consignor together with an accounting within            days of said sale.

5.      The Customer agrees to accept as full payment a commission equal to
        % of the gross sales price (exclusive of any sales tax), which the Customer shall collect and remit.

6.      The Customer agrees to permit the Consignor to enter the premises at reasonable times to examine and inspect the goods, and reconcile an accounting of sums due.

7.      Customer acknowledges that title to the goods shall remain with Consignor until goods are sold in the ordinary course of business.

8.      Risk of loss of the goods shall be the responsibility of Customer while said goods are within its possession.

9.     This agreement may be terminated by either party at will.  Upon termination all unsold goods shall be returned together with payment of any monies due.

10.     This agreement is not assignable and shall not be modified except by written modification.

11.     This agreement shall be binding upon and inure to the benefit of the parties, their successors, assigns and personal representatives.


_____     _____
Consignor                           Customer


Record in public filing office

# SALE ON APPROVAL

Date:

TO: _____
Customer

_____
Address

_____

Gentlemen:

We acknowledge the goods delivered on the attached invoice or order are sold on a <u>sale on approval</u> basis.

In the event you are not satisfied with the goods after inspection, you have the right to return the goods in merchantable condition at our expense within _____ days of receipt for full credit (or refund if prepaid). Goods not returned within that time shall be deemed accepted, and without further right of return. Until said goods are accepted we as seller shall retain title to said goods.

Upon acceptance, the balance of the purchase price shall be paid within the terms specified on the attached invoice. We thank you for your business and hope the goods will prove satisfactory and meet with your approval.

Very truly,

_____

# SALE OR RETURN

Date:

TO:_____

_____
Address

_____

Gentlemen:

The goods described on the attached order/invoice no.                    are sent

to you for examination or inspection only.

The goods remain our property and shall be returned to us on demand.  Title to the

goods does not pass until after a bill is rendered therefore.  Until returned you shall

assume responsibility for any damage or loss to the goods.  No right to sell, encumber or

otherwise dispose of the goods shall exist unless billed to you or consent given in writing.

Very truly,

_____

_____
Address

_____

# NOTICE OF DEFECTIVE GOODS

Date:

TO:_____
                    Supplier

_____
                    Address

_____

Gentlemen:

Please be advised we are in receipt of goods shipped to us under your invoice or

order number                           , dated                           , 19        .

Certain goods as listed on the attached sheet are defective or non-conforming to

our order for the following reasons:

Accordingly, we reject said goods and demand credit or adjustment in the amount

of $                          , representing the billed amount.  We also intend to re-ship said

goods to you at your expense.

Please confirm the credit and issue instructions for return of said goods.

You are advised by this notice that we reserve such further rights as we may have

under the Uniform Commercial Code or applicable law.

We look forward to your reply.

Very truly,

_____

# NOTICE OF REJECTION OF GOODS

Date: _____

TO: _____
                        Supplier

_____
                        Address

_____

Gentlemen:

Please be advised that on _____ , 19 _____ we received goods from

you on our purchase order or contract dated _____ , 19 _____ .

We hereby notify you of our intent to reject and return said goods for the reason(s)

checked below:

____ Goods were not delivered within time specified.

____ Goods were defective or damaged as described on reverse side.

____ Goods were non-conforming to sample, advertisement or specifications

       as stated on reverse side.

____ Acknowledged acceptance of our order, as required, has not been

       received, and we therefore ordered these goods from other sources.

____ Prices for said goods do not conform to quote, catalogue or order.

____ Goods represent only a partial shipment and we will not accept back order.

____ Other:

Please credit our account or refund if prepaid, and provide instructions for return of

said goods at your expense. Non-acceptance of these goods however shall not be a waiver

of any other claim we may have under the Uniform Commercial Code or applicable law.

We look forward to your reply.

Very truly,

_____

# ACKNOWLEDGED RECEIPT OF GOODS

Date:

TO:_____
         Supplier

     _____
         Address

     _____

The Undersigned hereby acknowledges receipt of goods from you

                              on date above, said goods identified by

invoice/shipping or packing slip no.        or Bill of Lading no.                    ,

and delivered by Supplier or

(Common Carrier).

The Undersigned acknowledges that it has been provided opportunity to fully

inspect said goods upon delivery and that said goods have been received in good

condition, free of visible defects or damage and in full conformity to our order with no

items missing or short except as may be specifically noted below:

In the presence of:

_____        _____
                                                        Customer

<u>Items (if any) damaged or short</u>

# WARRANTY BILL OF SALE

BE IT KNOWN, for good consideration, and in payment of the sum of

$                              , the receipt and sufficiency of which is acknowledged, the undersigned

(Seller) hereby sells and transfers to                              (Buyer) and its

successors and assigns forever, the following described chattels and personal property:

The Seller warrants to Buyer it has good and marketable title to said property, full

authority to sell and transfer said property, and that said property is sold free of all liens,

encumbrances, liabilities and adverse claims of every nature and description whatsoever.

Seller further warrants to Buyer that it will fully defend, protect, indemnify and hold

harmless the Buyer and its lawful successors and assigns from any adverse claim thereto.

Said assets are otherwise sold in "as is" condition and where presently located.

Signed under seal this            day of                              , 19        .

In the presence of:


_____          _____
                                         Seller


                                         _____
                                         Address

# BILL OF SALE WITH ENCUMBRANCES

BE IT KNOWN, for good consideration, and in payment of the sum of $

the receipt and sufficiency of which is acknowledged, the undersigned (Seller) hereby

sells and transfers to                                        (Buyer) and its successors and

assigns forever, the following described chattels and personal property:



The Seller warrants that it has good title to said property, but that said property is

being sold subject to a certain security interest, lien or encumbrance on said property in

favor of                                        (lienholder)

with a balance owed thereon of $

Buyer agrees to assume and punctually pay said secured debt and indemnify and

hold Seller harmless from any claim arising thereon.

Excepting only the encumbrance(s) specifically to be assumed by Buyer, the said

assets are otherwise sold free of other liens, encumbrances, liabilities or adverse claims

and Seller shall fully defend, indemnify and hold harmless the Buyer and its lawful

successors and assigns from any adverse claim thereto.  Said property is also sold "as is"

and where presently located.

Signed under seal this            day of                        , 19        .

In the presence of:


_____        _____
                                        Seller


                                        _____
                                        Address

# QUITCLAIM BILL OF SALE

BE IT KNOWN, for good consideration, and in consideration of the payment of

$                            , the receipt and sufficiency of which is acknowledged, the under-

signed (Seller) hereby sells, transfers, assigns and conveys unto

                    , and its successors and assigns forever with quitclaim covenants

only, the following described property:

Seller hereby sells and transfers only such right, title and interest as it may hold

and that said chattels sold herein are sold subject to such prior liens, encumbrances and

adverse claims, if any, that may exist, and Seller disclaims any and all warranties thereto.

Said assets are further sold in "as is" condition and where presently located.

Signed under seal this                    day of                         , 19        .

In the presence of:

_____          _____
                                          Seller

                                          _____
                                          Address

# BILL OF SALE
# FOR MOTOR VEHICLE

BE IT KNOWN, for good consideration, and in payment of the sum of $

the receipt and sufficiency of which is acknowledged, the undersigned (Seller) hereby

sells and transfers to                                              (Buyer) and its

successors and assigns the following described motor vehicle:

Make:

Model:

Year:

Vehicle Serial Number:

Color:

Seller warrants that it is the legal owner of said vehicle, that said vehicle is being

sold free and clear of all adverse claims, liens, and encumbrances, that Seller has full right

and authority to sell and transfer said vehicle, and Seller will protect, defend save

harmless, and indemnify Buyer from any adverse claims thereto.

Said vehicle is being sold "as is" without any express or implied warranty as to

condition or working order.

Signed under seal this                    day of                         , 19

In the presence of:


_____          _____
                                           Seller


                                           _____
                                           Address

# PURCHASE ORDER

| P.O. NUMBER | |
|---|---|
| DATE | DATE REQUIRED |
| TERMS | |
| SHIP VIA | |
| F.O.B. | |

**TO**
_____
_____
_____

**SHIP TO**
_____
_____
_____

| QTY. | UNIT | PLEASE SUPPLY ITEMS BELOW | UNIT PRICE | AMOUNT | |
|---|---|---|---|---|---|
| | | | | | |
| | | | | | |
| | | | | | |
| | | | | | |
| | | | | | |
| | | | | | |
| | | | | | |
| | | | | | |
| | | | | | |
| | | | | | |
| | | | | | |
| | | | | | |
| | | | | | |
| | | | | | |
| | | | | | |
| | | | | | |
| | | | | | |
| | | | | | |

**IMPORTANT**
This Purchase Order Number must appear on all invoices, acknowledgements, bills of lading, correspondence and shipping cartons.

Please notify us immediately if you are unable to ship complete order by date specified.
**STATE RESALE NUMBER**

_____

☐ RESALE      ☐ USE

Please send _____ copies of your invoice.

_____
**AUTHORIZED SIGNATURE**

# ASSIGNMENTS
# AND
# TRANSERS

7

# INVOICE

| | |
|---|---|
| INVOICE DATE | |
| OUR ORDER NO. | |
| YOUR ORDER NO. | |
| TERMS | F.O.B. |
| SALESMAN | |

| SHIPPED TO | SHIPPED VIA | PPD. or COLL. |
|---|---|---|
| | | |

| QUANTITY | DESCRIPTION | PRICE | AMOUNT |
|---|---|---|---|
| | | | |

# RETURN AUTHORIZATION

**SOLD TO**

CUSTOMER NO. _____

TERMS _____

SALES _____

APP. RTN. SHIP WEEK _____

**SHIP TO**

| COMPLETE FOR RETURN SHIPMENT AND INCLUDE A COPY OF THIS FORM AS PACKING LIST |
| --- |
| DATE SHIPPED |
| F.O.B. |
| ROUTING |

| YOUR ORDER NO. | ORDER DATE | OUR ORDER NO. |
| --- | --- | --- |
|  |  |  |

| ITEM | QUANTITY | DESCRIPTION | QUANTITY RECEIVED | UNIT PRICE | AMOUNT |
| --- | --- | --- | --- | --- | --- |
|  |  |  |  |  |  |

# RETURN AUTHORIZATION
**THIS FORM AUTHORIZES YOUR RETURN OF THE ABOVE ITEMS**

| DATE | TOTAL RETURN OF | |
| --- | --- | --- |
|  | ITEMS | DOLLAR AMOUNT |

| DATE | APPROVED BY | DATE | ITEMS RECEIVED OUR PLANT BY |
| --- | --- | --- | --- |
| DATE | APPROVED BY | DATE | ITEMS RECEIVED OUR PLANT BY |

# GENERAL ASSIGNMENT

BE IT KNOWN, for value received, the undersigned hereby unconditionally and irrevocably assigns, and transfers unto                                      all right, title and interest in and to the following:

The undersigned fully warrants that it has full rights and authority to enter into this assignment and transfer and that the rights and benefits assigned hereunder are free and clear of any lien, encumbrance, adverse claim or interest.

This assignment shall be binding upon and inure to the benefit of the parties, their successors, assigns and personal representatives.

Signed under seal this           day of                          , 19       .

In the presence of:

_____        _____
                                        Assignor

_____        _____
                                        Assignee

# ASSIGNMENT OF ACCOUNTS RECEIVABLE

BE IT KNOWN, for value received, the undersigned hereby unconditionally and irrevocably sells, transfers and conveys all right, title and interest in and to the account(s) receivable as annexed, to                                          (Assignee) and its successors and assigns.

The undersigned warrants that the said account(s) are just and due in the amounts stated and the undersigned has not received payment for same or any part thereof and has no knowledge of any dispute or defense thereon, provided, however, that said account(s) are sold without guaranty or warranty of collection and without recourse to the undersigned in the event of non-payment.  Assignee may prosecute collection of any receivable in its own name.

The undersigned further warrants that it has full title to said receivables, full authority to sell and transfer same, and that said receivables are sold free and clear of all liens, encumbrances or adverse claims.

This agreement shall be binding upon and inure to the benefit of the parties, their successors, assigns and personal representatives.

Signed under seal this                day of                                , 19        .


_____

In the presence of:


_____

# ASSIGNMENT OF CONTRACT

BE IT KNOWN, for value received, the undersigned Assignor hereby assigns,

transfers and sets over to                                    (Assignee) all

right, title and interest held by the Assignor in and to the following described contract with

dated                              , 19    :

The Assignor hereby warrants and represents that said contract is in full force and

effect in the form and on the terms annexed and said contract is fully assignable.

The Assignee hereby assumes and agrees to perform all the remaining and

executory obligations of the Assignor under the contract, if any, and agrees to indemnify

and hold the Assignor harmless from any claim or demand resulting from non-performance

therein by the Assignee.  The Assignee shall be entitled to all monies and other benefits

accrued or remaining to be paid under the contract, which rights are also assigned here-

under.  The Assignor further warrants that it has full right and authority to transfer said

contract and that the contract rights herein transferred are free of lien, encumbrance,

adverse claim or notice that said contract is other than in good standing.

This assignment shall be binding upon and inure to the benefit of the parties,

their successors, assigns and personal representatives.

Signed under seal this              day of                        , 19     .

In the presence of:


_____          _____
                                          Assignor


_____          _____
                                          Assignee

# ASSIGNMENT OF COPYRIGHT OR TRADEMARK

BE IT KNOWN, the undersigned                            of

(Owner) being the lawful Owner of a certain

copyright or trademark registered in the United States Patent Office under registration

number                            , dated                            , 19            , for good

consideration does hereby sell, transfer, assign and convey all right, title and interest in

said Copyright or Trademark and all rights and goodwill attaching thereto unto

(Buyer).  A fascimile of said Copyright or Trademark is annexed.

The Owner warrants that said Copyright or Trademark is in full force and good

standing and there is no other assignment of rights or licenses granted under said Copy-

right or Trademark or known infringements by or against said Copyright or Trademark.

Owner further warrants that he is the lawful Owner of said Copyright or Trademark,

that it has full right and authority to transfer said Copyright or Trademark and that said Copy-

right or Trademark is transferred free and clear of all liens, encumbrances and adverse

claims thereto, and that the owner shall sign such other documents required to transfer

same.

This agreement shall be binding upon and inure to the benefit of the parties, their

successors, assigns and personal representatives.

Signed under seal this            day of                            , 19            .

_____

Note: Delete words that do not apply

State of

, SS.

County of                                                                    , 19            .

Then personally appeared

who acknowledged the foregoing, before me

_____

Notary Public

My Commission Expires:

# ASSIGNMENT OF DAMAGE CLAIM

BE IT KNOWN, for value received, the undersigned hereby unconditionally and irrevocably assigns and transfers unto          (Assignee) and its successors, assigns and personal representatives, any and all claims, demands, and cause or causes of action of any kind whatsoever which the undersigned has or may have against          arising from the following:

The Assignee may in its own name, at its own expense, and for its own benefit prosecute said claim and collect, settle, compromise and grant releases on said claim as it in its sole discretion deems advisable, provided the undersigned shall reasonably assist and cooperate in the prosecution of said claim to the extent required or requested. Assignee shall be entitled to all judgments, awards and payments thereon.

The undersigned warrants it has full right and authority to assign this claim and that said claim is free and clear of any lien, encumbrance or other adverse interest. Assignor disclaims any representation as to the merits or collectability of such claim.

This assignment shall be binding upon and inure to the benefit of the parties, their successors, assigns and personal representatives.

Signed under seal this      day of          , 19    .

In the presence of:

_____    _____

# ASSIGNMENT OF INCOME

BE IT KNOWN, for value received, the undersigned hereby irrevocably and

unconditionally assigns and transfers to                                        (Assignee)

all rights to income, rentals, fees, profits, dividends or monies that is now or shall

hereinafter be due the undersigned from                                        arising

from the following obligation:

The undersigned warrants that there are no known setoffs or defenses to the

payments due.  The undersigned further warrants that said obligation to pay is absolute

and without modification.  The undersigned further warrants it has full authority to enter

into this agreement and that the rights to income assigned hereunder are free and clear of

liens, encumbrances and adverse claim.  The undersigned does not, however, guarantee

or warranty the collectability of any monies due.  This assignment shall be limited to

$                        and no greater amount.

This assignment shall be binding upon and inure to the benefit of the parties, and

their successors, assigns and personal representatives.

Signed under seal this            day of                        , 19        .

In the presence of:

_____        _____

# ASSIGNMENT OF INSURANCE POLICY

BE IT KNOWN, for value received, the undersigned hereby irrevocably transfers and assigns all legal and beneficial right, title and interest in and to the within policy of insurance standing in my name known as policy no.                    issued by

(Insurance Company) together with all cash values, proceeds and benefits thereto arising, subject to the conditions of said policy and the requirements of the issuing company.

The undersigned warrants that it has full authority to transfer said policy, and shall execute all documents as may be required.

This assignment shall be binding upon and inure to the benefit of the parties, their successors, assigns and personal representatives.

Signed under seal this            day of                        , 19      .


_____

# NOTICE OF ASSIGNMENT

Date:

TO:_____

_____
**Address**

_____

You are hereby notified that on _____ , 19 ___ , we have

assigned and transferred to _____ , the following

existing between us:

Please direct any further correspondence (or payments, if applicable) to them at

the following address:

_____

_____

_____

Please contact us if you have any questions.

_____

_____
**Address**

_____

# PERSONAL
# AND
# FAMILY

_____

8

# COHABITATION AGREEMENT

BE IT KNOWN, this agreement is made this          day of                                  ,

19       , by                                        and

who presently reside in the State of                         .

1.      Relationship: The parties wish to live together in a relationship similar to

matrimony but do not wish to be bound by the statutory or common-law provisions relating

to marriage.

2.      Duration of Relationship: It is agreed that we will live together for an indefinite

period of time subject to the following terms:

3.      Property: Any real or personal property acquired by us or either of us during the

relationship shall be considered to be our separate property.  All property listed on the

pages attached is made a part of this agreement by this reference.  The property now and

hereinafter belongs to the party under whose name it is listed prior to the making of this

agreement.  All listed property is and shall continue to be the separate property of the

person who now owns it.  All property received by either of us by gift or inheritance during

our relationship shall be the separate property of the one who receives it.

4.      Income: All income of either of us and all our accumulations during the existence

of our relationship shall be maintained in one fund.  Our debts and expenses arising

during the existence of our union shall be paid out of this fund.  Each of us shall have an

equal interest in this sum, and equal right to its management and control, and be equally

entitled to the surplus remaining after payment of all debts and expenses.

5.      Termination: Our relationship may be terminated at the sole will and decision of

either of us, expressed by a written notice given to the other.

6.      Modification of This Agreement: This agreement may be modified by any

agreement in writing by both parties, with the exception that no modifications may

decrease the obligations that may be imposed regarding any children born of our union.

7. <u>Application of Law</u>: The validity of this agreement shall be determined solely under the laws of the State of                               as they may from time to time be changed.

8. Neither party shall maintain any action or claim as against the other for support, alimony, compensation or for rights to any property existing prior to this date, or acquired during or subsequent to the date of termination.

9. The parties enter into this agreement of their own will and accord without reliance on any other inducement or promise.

10. Each party to this agreement has had the opportunity to have this agreement reviewed by independent counsel.

Signed under seal this            day of                          , 19       .

_____

_____

# RELEASE OF COHABITATION CLAIMS

1.　　Parties: This mutual cohabitation release agreement is entered into this

day of　　　　　　　　　, 19　　, by

and　　　　　　　　　　　　　　　.

2.　　Relationship: We want to live together, without benefit of marriage, but do not want to acquire any rights or obligations with respect to property, income, or support that might otherwise come to either of us by reason of this non-marital relationship.

3.　　Terms of Release: We give our mutual and complete releases to each other, and we waive all rights or interest in the property or income of the other that might in any way arise during our relationship or because of our relationship or rendition of services to each other. We specifically waive all rights to support and maintenance that may arise from our association. We further waive all rights to all assets or property that the other party owns at the date of this Agreement.

4.　　We acknowledge we have not entered into any other agreement or relied on any promise or inducement for purposes of entering into this relationship.

5.　　This release shall be binding upon and inure to the benefit of the parties, their successors, assigns, and personal representatives.

　　　　　Signed under seal this　　　　　　day of　　　　　　　　　　, 19　　.


In the presence of:


_____　　_____


_____　　_____

# PRE-MARITAL AGREEMENT

BE IT KNOWN, this agreement is entered into on the          day of

          ,19     , between                         and                         .

Whereas, the parties contemplate legal marriage under the laws of the State of

          , and it is their mutual desire to enter into this agreement so that they will

continue to own and control their own property, and are getting married because of their

love for each other but do not desire that their present respective financial interests be

changed by their marriage.  Now, therefore, it is agreed as follows:

1.       All property which belongs to each of the above parties shall be, and shall forever

remain, their personal estate, including all interest, rents, and profits which may accrue

from said property, and said property shall remain forever free of claim by the other.

2.       The parties shall have at all times the full right and authority, in all respects the

same as each would have if not married, to use, sell, enjoy, manage, gift and convey all

property as may presently belong to him or her.

3.       In the event of a separation or divorce, the parties shall have no right against each

other by way of claims for support, alimony, maintenance, compensation or division of

property existing of this date.

4.       In the event of separation or divorce, marital property acquired after marriage shall

nevertheless remain subject to division, either by agreement or judicial determination.

5.       This agreement shall be binding upon and inure to the benefit of the parties, their

successors, assigns and personal representatives.

          This agreement shall be enforced in accordance with the laws of the State

of                         .

          Signed under seal this          day of                         , 19     .

Witnessed:

_____   _____


_____   _____

# POSTNUPTIAL PROPERTY AGREEMENT

This agreement made by and between

(Husband) and                                      (Wife) who have been married since

, 19        , and who reside at

, County of                                    , State of

This agreement is entered into with the intent and desire to specify and define the respective rights of the parties in and to the separate, joint and community property of the parties but with the express understanding that neither party wishes to obtain a divorce or legal separation.

Now, therefore, it is hereby stipulated by the parties that:

1.      The Husband shall have sole and exclusive rights to the described personal and real property listed on Exhibit A, notwithstanding whether said property is presently held by Husband and Wife, jointly or as community property or other co-tenancy.

2.      The Wife shall have sole and exclusive rights to the described personal and real property listed on Exhibit B, notwithstanding whether said property is presently held by Wife and Husband, jointly or as community property or other co-tenancy.

3.      All property stipulated to be property of one or the other parties shall be taken subject to all present or future liens, mortgages, encumbrances or claims of record.

4.      The parties shall from time to time stipulate the respective rights to marital property acquired from and after the date of this agreement.

5.      All exhibits are herein incorporated by reference.

6.      The parties agree to execute all documents necessary to perfect good title to the respective properties to the named spouse.

7.      Both parties acknowledge that they have either been represented by seperate counsel or had full opportunity to be so represented.

8. This agreement shall be binding upon and inure to the benefit of the parties, their successors, assigns and personal representatives.

Signed under seal this       day of       , 19   .

_____

_____

State of

County of       , SS.       , 19   .

Then personally appeared       , and

, who acknowledged the foregoing,

before me.

_____

Notary Public

My Commission Expires:

# SEPARATION AGREEMENT

This agreement is made between                          (Husband)

who resides at                                    and

(Wife) who resides at

1.      Date of Marriage: The parties were married on                    , 19    ,

in the State of                    and have last resided within the State of

2.      Reasons for Separation: Due to irreconcilable differences, the parties separated

on                    , 19    , and have been living apart since that date, and desire to

remain apart hereafter.

3.      Children of Marriage: No children where born of this marriage.

4.      Conduct of the Parties: The parties agree they shall continue to live apart for the

rest of their lives.  Each shall be free from interference, direct or indirect, by the other as

fully as though never married.  Each spouse may, for his or her separate benefit, engage

in any employment, business, or profession or engage in such social activity that he or

she may choose.  The parties shall not molest or bother each other or interfere with their

activities.

5.      Property settlement: The parties have divided their property to their mutual

satisfaction with each party entitled to the specific assets identified on the annexed

schedules, and neither party shall make claim to the assets of the other.

6.      Debts: Husband and Wife agree that they are no longer liable for the debts of the

other and each will take reasonable steps to prevent the other from being billed for his or

her debts and shall indemnify and hold harmless said spouse for any claims thereto. The

marital debts that each party shall assume and pay are annexed.

7.      Alimony: The parties agree that neither of them shall be required to provide

maintenance, alimony or support payment to the other.  The parties further agree that neither of them shall now or hereafter seek alimony or support in any court as each are fully capable of their independent support.

8. The parties agree to enter this agreement as a stipulation or decree in any court of competent jurisdiction and agree to be bound by its provisions in any divorce or other judicial proceeding.

9. Each party acknowledges that he or she entered into this agreement of their own free will and there are no other terms, conditions or inducements except as contained herein. Each party has had full opportunity to have this agreement reviewed by their own counsel.

10. This agreement shall be binding upon and inure to the benefit of the parties, their successors, assigns and personal representatives.

Signed under seal this          day of                    , 19    .

In the presence of:

_____        _____
                                   Husband


_____        _____
                                   Wife

# GENERAL POWER OF ATTORNEY

TO ALL PERSONS, be it known, that

the undersigned Grantor, does hereby grant a general power of attorney to

, as my attorney-in-fact.

My attorney-in-fact shall have full powers and authority to do and undertake all acts on my behalf that I could do personally including but not limited to the right to sell, deed, buy, trade, lease, mortgage, assign, rent or dispose of any of my present or future real or personal property; the right to execute, accept, undertake and perform any and all contracts in my name; the right to deposit, endorse, or withdraw funds to or from any of my bank accounts, depositories or safe deposit box; the right to borrow, lend, invest or reinvest funds on any terms; the right to initiate, defend, commence or settle legal actions on my behalf; the right to vote (in person or by proxy) any shares or beneficial interest in any entity, and the right to retain any accountant, attorney or other advisor deemed necessary to protect my interests generally or relative to any foregoing unlimited power.

My attorney-in-fact hereby accepts this appointment subject to its terms and agrees to act and perform in said fiduciary capacity consistent with my best interests as he in his best discretion deems advisable, and I affirm and ratify all acts so undertaken.

This power of attorney may be revoked by me at any time, and shall automatically be revoked upon my death, provided any person relying on this power of attorney before or after my death shall have full rights to accept the authority of my attorney-in-fact until in receipt of actual notice of revocation.

Signed under seal this           day of                    , 19      .

_____
Grantor

_____
Attorney-in-Fact

Note: Delete powers that do not apply

State of

County of      , SS.                  , 19  .

   Then personally appeared              and

   , who acknowledged the foregoing, before me.

_____

Notary Public

My Commission Expires:

# LIMITED POWER OF ATTORNEY

TO ALL PERSONS, be it known, that I,                                        , of

                              , as Grantor, do hereby grant a limited and

specific power of attorney to                              , of

                    , as my attorney-in-fact.

My named attorney-in-fact shall have full power and authority to undertake and

perform the following acts on my behalf to the same extent as if I had done so personally:

The authority granted shall include such incidental acts as are reasonably  required

or necessary to carry out and perform the specific authorities and duties stated herein.

My attorney-in-fact agrees to accept this appointment subject to its terms, and

agrees to act and perform in said fiduciary capacity consistent with my best interests as he

in his discretion deems advisable, and I ratify all acts so carried out.

This power of attorney may be revoked by me at any time, and shall automatically

be revoked upon my death, provided any person relying on this power of attorney before

or after my death shall have full rights to accept the authority of my attorney-in-fact con-

sistent with the powers granted until in receipt of actual notice of revocation.

Signed under seal this                    day of                    , 19     .


_____
Grantor


_____
Attorney-in-Fact

State of _____ , 19 ___ .

, SS.

County of _____

Then personally appeared _____ and

_____ , who acknowledged the foregoing, before me.

_____

Notary Public

My Commission Expires:

# DURABLE POWER OF ATTORNEY

BE IT KNOWN, that                                              , the

undersigned Grantor, does hereby grant a durable power of attorney to

, as my attorney-in-fact.

My attorney-in-fact shall have full powers and authority to do and undertake all

acts on my behalf that I could do personally including but not limited to the right to sell,

deed, buy, trade, lease, mortgage, assign, rent or dispose of any real or personal

property; the right to execute, accept, undertake and perform all contracts in my name;

the right to deposit, endorse, or withdraw funds to or from any of my bank accounts or

safe deposit box; the right to borrow, collect, lend, invest or reinvest funds; the right to

initiate, defend, commence or settle legal actions on my behalf; the right to vote (in

person or by proxy) any shares or beneficial interest in any entity, and the right to retain

any accountant, attorney or other advisor deemed necessary to protect my interests

relative to any foregoing unlimited power.  My attorney-in-fact shall have full power to

execute, deliver and accept all documents and undertake all acts consistent with the

foregoing.

This power of attorney shall become effective upon and remain in effect only

during such time periods as I may be mentally or physically incapacitated and unable to

care for my own needs or make competent decisions as are necessary to protect my

interests or conduct my affairs.

My attorney-in-fact hereby accepts this appointment subject to its terms and

agrees to act and perform in said fiduciary capacity consistent with my best interests as he

in his best discretion deems advisable, and I affirm and ratify all acts so undertaken.

This power of attorney may be revoked by me at any time, and shall automatically

be revoked upon my death, provided any person relying on this power of attorney shall have full rights to accept the authority of my attorney-in-fact until in receipt of actual notice of revocation.

Signed under seal this                   day of                                   , 19        .

_____

State of                                                                                          , 19        .
                                          , SS.
County of

Then personally appeared                                                                        ,

who acknowledged the foregoing, before me.

_____

Notary Public

My Commission Expires:

# DURABLE POWER OF ATTORNEY
# FOR HEALTH CARE

BE IT KNOWN that                                                      , the undersigned Grantor, does hereby grant a durable power of attorney for health care to                                      , as my attorney-in-fact.

I hereby grant to my Agent full power and authority to make health care decisions for me to the same extent that I could make such decisions for myself if I had the capacity to do so. In exercising this authority, my Agent shall make health care decisions that are consistent with my desires as stated in this document or otherwise make known to my Agent, including, but not limited to, my desires concerning obtaining or refusing or withdrawing life prolonging care, treatment, services, and procedures.

I hereby authorize all physicians and psychiatrists who have treated me, and all other providers of health care, including hospitals, to release to my Agent all information contained in my medical records which my Agent may request. I hereby waive all privileges attached to physician-patient relationship and to any communication, verbal or written, arising out of such a relationship. My Agent is authorized to request, receive and review any information, verbal or written, pertaining to my physical or mental health, including medical and hospital records, and to execute any releases, waivers or other documents that may be required in order to obtain such information, and to disclose such information to such persons, organizations and health care providers as my Agent shall deem appropriate. My Agent is authorized to employ and discharge health care providers including physicians, psychiatrists, dentists, nurses, and therapists as my Agent shall deem appropriate for my physical, mental and emotional well-being. My Agent is also authorized to pay reasonable fees and expenses for such services contracted.

My Agent is authorized to apply for my admission to a medical, nursing, residential or other similar facility, execute any consent or admission forms required by such facility and enter into agreements for my care at such facility or elsewhere during my lifetime. My Agent is authorized to arrange for and consent to medical, therapeutical and surgical procedures for me including the administration of drugs. The power to make health care decisions for me shall include the power to give consent, refuse consent, or withdraw consent to any care, treatment, service, or procedure to maintain, diagnose, or treat a physical or mental condition.

I reserve unto myself the right to revoke the authority granted to my Agent hereunder to make health care decisions for me by notifying the treating physician, hospital, or other health care provider orally or in writing. Notwithstanding any provision herein to the contrary, I retain the right to make medical and other health care decisions for myself so long as I am able to give informed consent with respect to a particular decision. In addition, no treatment may be given to me over my objection, and health care necessary to keep me alive may not be stopped if I object.

This power of attorney shall not be affected by subsequent disability or incapacity of the principal. Notwithstanding any provision herein to the contrary, my Agent shall take no action under this instrument unless I am deemed to be disabled or incapacitated as defined herein. My incapacity shall be deemed to exist when so certified in writing by two licensed physicians not related by blood or marriage to either me or to my Agent. The said certificate shall state that I am incapable of caring for myself and that I am physically and mentally incapable of managing my financial affairs. The certificate of the physicians described above shall be attached to the original of this instrument and if this instrument is filed or recorded among public records, then such certificate shall also be similarly filed or recorded if permitted by applicable law.

My Agent shall be entitled to reimbursement for all reasonable costs actually incurred and paid by my Agent on my behalf under the authority granted in this instrument.

To the extent permitted by law, I herewith nominate, constitute and appoint my Agent to serve as my guardian, conservator and/or in any similar representative capacity, and, if I am not permitted by law to so nominate, constitute and appoint, then I request any court of competent jurisdiction which may be petitioned by any person to appoint a guardian, conservator or similar representative for me to give due consideration to my request.

Signed this                day of                                    , 19        .


_____


State of                                                                                  , 19        .

                               , SS.

County of


Then personally appeared                                                                    ,

who acknowledged the foregoing, before me.


_____

Notary Public

My Commission Expires:

# REVOCATION OF POWER OF ATTORNEY

TO:_____

_____
          Address

_____

    I hereby make reference to a certain power of attorney granted by me

                  , as Grantor to you                ,

as my Attorney-in-Fact, and dated          , 19   .

    This document acknowledges that as Grantor I hereby revoke, rescind and

terminate said power-of-attorney and all authority, rights and power thereto effective this

date.

    Please acknowledge receipt of this revocation and return said acknowledged

copy to me.

    Signed under seal this           day of           , 19   .

_____
Grantor

State of

                  , SS.                  , 19   .

County of

    Then personally appeared                  ,

who as Grantor acknowledged the foregoing, before me.

_____
Notary Public

My Commission Expires:

Acknowledged:

_____
Attorney-in-Fact

# LIVING WILL

Directive to my physicians, my attorneys, my clergyman, my family or others responsiblle for my health, welfare or affairs made this _____ day of _____ 19 ___ .

I, _____ , of _____ , State of _____ , being of sound mind, willfully and voluntarily make known my desire that my life shall not be artificially prolonged under the circumstances set forth below and do hereby declare that, if at any time I should have an incurable injury, disease or illness certified to be a terminal condition by two physicians and where the application of life-sustaining procedures would serve only to artificially prolong the moment of my death and where my physician determines that my death is imminent or needlessly prolonged whether or not life-sustaining procedures are utilized, I direct that such procedures be withheld or withdrawn and that I be permitted to die naturally with only the merciful administration of medication to eliminate or reduce pain to my mind and body or the performance of any medical procedure deemed necessary to provide me with comfort care.  In the absence of my ability to give directions regarding the use of such life-sustaining procedures, it is my intention that this directive shall be honored by my family and physician(s) as the final expression of my legal right to refuse medical or surgical treatment and I accept the consequences from such refusal.  If I have bequeathed organs, I ask that I be kept alive for a sufficient time to enable the proper withdrawal and transplant of said organs.

_____

The declarer has been personally known to me and I believe said declarer to be of sound mind.

_____     _____
Witness                            Address


_____     _____
Witness                            Address

# GIFT UNDER UNIFORM ANATOMICAL GIFT ACT

I, _____ (Donor) being of sound mind

and being at least 18 years of age, do hereby give my _____
                                                        Organ or part of body

to_____of_____
                                              Address

_____, City of_____, County of_____,

State of_____. This gift will be effective immediately following my

death, and I authorize my physicians to carry out this gift in such manner as they deem

medically proper.

Dated:_____, 19____.

_____

Donor

_____

Address

_____

_____

Date of Birth

The above-named donor signed this document in our presence, and we now sign

as witnesses in the donor's presence, and in the presence of each other.

_____          _____

Witness                                     Witness

_____          _____

Address                                     Address

# DONOR CARD

of_____
Print or Type Name of Donor

In the hope that I may help others, I hereby make this anatomical gift, if medically

acceptable, for the purposes of transplantation, to take effect upon my death.

The words and marks below indicate my desires:

I give:   a) _____ any needed organs

b) _____ only the following organs for purposes of transplantation,
therapy, education or medical research:

c) _____ my entire body, for anatomical or medical study, if needed

Limitations or special wishes:

Signed by the donor and following two witnesses, preferrably next of kin, in the

presence of each other.

_____      _____
Signature of Donor                    Birthdate

_____      _____
Date Signed                           City and State

_____      _____
Witness                               Witness

### THIS IS A LEGAL DOCUMENT UNDER THE ANATOMICAL GIFT ACT.

UNIFORM DONOR CARD

of _____
Print or type name of donor

In the hope that I may help others, I hereby make this anatomical gift, if medically acceptable, for the purposes of transplantation, to take effect upon my death.
The words and marks below indicate my desires.

I give: (a) _____ any needed organs
(b)_____only the following organs

_____
Specify the organ(s)

(c)_____my entire body for study if needed.
Additional forms needed for whole body donation.
PUT IN WALLET BY DRIVER'S LICENSE OR I.D.

Signed by the donor and following two witnesses, preferably next of kin, in presence of each other.

_____
SIGNATURE OF DONOR          Birthdate of Donor

_____
Date Signed                 City and State

_____
Witness

_____
Witness

_____
This is a legal document under the Uniform Anatomical Gift Act.

# REVOCATION OF ANATOMICAL GIFT

To my physicians, clergy, attorney, family and prospective donees whether named or unnamed.

BE IT KNOWN, on _____, 19 ___, the undersigned entered into an anatomical gift to take effect upon my death.

Effective immediately, I hereby revoke and cancel said gift and provide that no prior gift under the Uniform Anatomical Gift Act shall be of force and effect.

Signed under seal this _____ day of _____, 19 ___ .

In the presence of:

_____        _____
                                        Donor

                                        _____
                                        Address

                                        _____

# GIFT TO MINOR
## UNDER UNIFORM GIFT TO MINORS ACT

I,                                          (Donor) of

deliver to                                  of

as Custodian (Name) for

(Beneficiary) the following described property:

This delivery constitutes an unrestricted and irrevocable gift of said property to

the Beneficiary under the Uniform Gift to Minors Act of the State of

The Custodian shall have all manner of right to invest, reinvest, buy, trade, vote,

deal with and otherwise exercise all form of powers of the gift property on behalf of the

Beneficiary and upon said Beneficiary reaching majority age shall deliver said property (or

substituted property) with all accrued profits or earnings to said Beneficiary.  The

Custodian is to serve without bond.

Dated:                              _____
                                    Donor


                                    _____
                                    Custodian

# GIFT DECLARATION

BE IT ACKNOWLEDGED, that I/we

(Donor) hereby make a non-revocable gift of the below described property to

and his or her successors and assigns forever,

and by this instrument give, transfer, and convey full right, title and interest to same.

This gift shall not be considered an advance towards any testamentary gift or

bequest I may make to the aforesaid under any will, but shall be construed as an

independent undertaking.

Signed and effective this                 day of                         , 19        .

In the presence of:

_____        _____
                                       Donor

Property:

## DONEE'S ACKNOWLEDGEMENT

I,                                       accept the above gift and

acknowledge receipt of the original of the above declaration and physical possession of

the above gift.

_____
                                       Donee

# GIFT IN ADVANCE OF
# TESTAMENTARY BEQUEST

BE IT KNOWN that I                                    of

do hereby gift, transfer

and convey to                              the below described property:

It is further acknowledged that this shall be considered an advance against any

testamentary bequest I may choose to make to said donee under any last will and

testament and therefore said gift having a stipulated value of $          shall be

so deducted from any future testamentary bequest.

Signed under seal this          day of                    , 19      .

In the presence of:

_____          _____

# AUTHORIZATION TO RELEASE
# MEDICAL INFORMATION

Date:

TO:_____

_____
Address

_____

I hereby authorize and request that you release and deliver to:




all my medical records, charts, files, prognoses, reports, x-rays, laboratory reports and

such other information relative to my medical condition or my treatment at any time

provided to me and all to the extent said information is available and within your

possession. You may bill me for any costs. You are further requested not to disclose any

information concern-ing my past or present medical condition to any other person without

my express written permission.

Thank you for your cooperation.


In the presence of:


_____    _____
                             Name


                             _____
                             Address

# AGREEMENT THAT EARNINGS
# REMAIN SEPARATE PROPERTY

BE IT KNOWN, for good consideration,

(Husband) and                                          (Wife) enter into this agreement.

The Husband and Wife were married on                              , 19        , in

                                        . As of the date of this agreement

they remain living together as Husband and Wife.

The below signed Husband and Wife further agree, however, that their respective earnings or income from any employment in which they may engage during the course of their marriage shall remain the exclusive property of the person who earned it, and shall not become community property.

Signed under seal this              day of                            , 19        .

_____

_____

State of                                                            , 19        .

                              , SS.

County of

Then personally appeared                                          and

                    , who acknowledged the foregoing, before me.

_____
Notary Public

My Commission Expires:

# AGREEMENT TO CONVERT SEPARATE PROPERTY INTO COMMUNITY PROPERTY

BE IT KNOWN, for good consideration,

(Husband) and                                              (Wife) acknowledge that during the

course of their marriage they have acquired property which by the laws of the State of

, is community property.  A list of said community property is annexed

as Exhibit A.

Husband and Wife further acknowledge that any property now held individually is

annexed as Exhibit B and is hereby deemed to be community property.

Husband and Wife further agree that all after-acquired property, whether

individually or collectively held shall be deemed community property of the parties.

This agreement shall be binding upon and inure to the benefit of the parties, their

successors, assigns and personal representatives.

Signed under seal this                day of                              , 19       .


_____
Husband

_____
Wife


State of

, SS.                                              , 19       .

County of


Then personally appeared                                              and

, who acknowledged the foregoing, before me.


_____
Notary Public

My Commission Expires:

# OTHER
# LEGAL FORMS

9

# ARBITRATION AGREEMENT

Agreement by and between                                                                                        and

Be it acknowledged, that we the undersigned as our interests exist in and to a

certain contract, dispute, controversy, action or claim described as:

(claim) do hereby agree to resolve any dispute or controversy we now have or may ever

have in connection with or arising from said claim by binding Arbitration.

Said Arbitration shall be in accordance with the rules and procedures of the

American Arbitration Association for the City of                                                  , which rules

and procedures for arbitration are incorporated herein by reference and the decision or

award by the Arbitrators shall be final, conclusive and binding upon each of us and

enforceable in a court of law of proper jurisdiction.

Signed this                                    day of                                          , 19            .

In the presence of:

_____          _____


_____          _____

# CONFIDENTIALITY AND
# TRADE SECRET AGREEMENT

AGREEMENT by and between

(Company) and                                                                          (Undersigned).

Whereas, the Company agrees to allow the Undersigned access to certain

confidential information, trade secrets or proprietory information relating to the affairs of

the Company only for purposes of:



                                                                                                                   , and

Whereas, the Undersigned may  review, examine, inspect, have access to or

obtain such information only for the purposes described above, and to otherwise hold

such disclosed information confidential pursuant to the terms of this agreement.

BE IT ACKNOWLEDGED, that the Company has or shall furnish to the Under-

signed certain confidential information, described on the attached list, and Company may

further allow the Undersigned the right to inspect the business of the Company and/or

interview suppliers, customers, employees or representatives of the Company, only on

the following conditions:

1.      The Undersigned agrees to hold all disclosed confidential or proprietory

information or trade secrets ("information") in trust and confidence and agrees that it shall

be used only for the contemplated purpose, and shall not be used for any other purpose

nor disclosed to any third party without written consent of Company.

2.      No copies or abstracts will be made or retained of any written information

supplied.  Upon demand by the Company, all information, including written notes,

photographs, or memoranda shall be returned to the Company.

3.      The disclosed information shall not be disclosed to any employee, consultant or third party unless said party agrees to execute and be bound by the terms of this agreement.

4.      It is understood that the Undersigned shall have no obligation to hold confidential with respect to any information known by the Undersigned or generally known within the industry prior to date of this agreement, or that shall become common knowledge within the industry thereafter as said information shall not be deemed protected under this agreement.

5.      The Undersigned acknowledges the information disclosed herein as proprietory and trade secrets and in the event of any breach, the Company shall be entitled to injuctive relief as a cumulative and not necessarily successive remedy without need to post bond.

6.      This agreement shall be binding upon and inure to the benefit of the parties, their successors, assigns and personal representatives.


Signed under seal this          day of                          , 19      .


In the presence of:


_____          _____


_____          _____

# INDEMNIFICATION AGREEMENT

BE IT KNOWN, for value received, the undersigned Indemnitors jointly and severally agree to fully and unconditionally indemnify, defend and hold harmless

(Indemnitees) and its

successors and assigns, from any loss, liability, claim, action, or suit, arising from or incurred in connection with the following:

Upon any such asserted claim, the Indemnitees shall provide each of the undersigned reasonably timely written notice of said claim. The undersigned shall thereafter at its own expense pay or satisfy said claim or otherwise defend, protect and hold harmless Indemnitees against said claim or any loss or liability thereunder.

However, in the future event the undersigned shall fail to promptly and reasonably defend and/or indemnify and hold harmless the Indemnitees, then in such instance the Indemnitees shall have full rights to defend, pay or settle said claim on their own behalf with notice to the undersigned and thereafter Indemnitees shall have full rights or recourse against the undersigned to be reimbursed for all fees, costs, expenses and payments reasonably required to be paid to discharge and defend against said claim.

Upon any breach of this Agreement, the undersigned further agrees to pay all reasonable attorneys' fees necessary to enforce this agreement. This agreement shall be unlimited as to amount or duration.

This agreement shall be binding upon and inure to the benefit of the parties, their successors, assigns and personal representatives.

Signed under seal this                    day of                              , 19        .

Witnesseth:


_____          _____
                                         Indemnitor


_____          _____
                                         Indemnitor

# NON-COMPETITION AGREEMENT

BE IT KNOWN, FOR GOOD AND VALUABLE CONSIDERATION, the Undersigned jointly and severally agree not to compete with the business of

(Company) and its lawful successors, assigns and affiliates in accordance with the terms herein.

The term "not compete" as used herein shall mean that the Undersigned shall not directly or indirectly on his own behalf or on behalf of others engage in a business or other commercial activity described as:

notwithstanding whether as an owner, officer, director, lender, investor, employee, agent, consultant, partner or stockholder (excepting as a minority stockholder in a publicly owned company).

This covenant and agreement shall extend only for a radius of            miles from the present location of the Company at

and shall remain in full force and effect only for            years from date hereof at which time this agreement shall expire.

In the event of any violation of this agreement, the Company shall be entitled to full equitable and injunctive relief without need to post bond or surety, which rights shall be cumulative with and not necessarily successive or exclusive of any other legal rights to monetary damages that the company may have.

This agreement shall be binding upon and inure to the benefit of the parties, their successors, assigns and personal representatives.

Signed under seal this            day of            , 19      .

Witnesseth:

_____    _____

_____    _____

# PERSONAL PROPERTY RENTAL AGREEMENT

AGREEMENT made between

(Owner) and                                              (Renter):

1.      Owner hereby rents to renter the below described personal property:

2.      Renter shall pay Owner the sum of $                    as payment for the

rental herein, said sum paid as follows:

3.      The Renter shall during the rental term keep and maintain the property in good

condition and repair and shall be responsible for all loss, casualty, damage or destruction

to said property notwithstanding how caused and Renter agrees to return said property in

the same condition as when rented, reasonable wear and tear expected.

4.      The Renter shall not during the rental period allow others use of the property or

re-let said property to others.

5.      The rental period shall commence on                         , 19      and

terminate on                         , 19      , at which date the property shall be

promptly returned.

6.      Other terms:

Signed under seal this                day of                         , 19      .

_____

_____

# ADDENDUM TO CONTRACT

Reference is made to a certain agreement by and between the undersigned parties, said agreement being dated _____ , 19_____ ("Contract").

BE IT KNOWN, that for good consideration the parties made the following additions or changes a part of said agreement as if contained therein:

Signed under seal this _____ day of _____ , 19_____

_____

_____

# EXTENSION OF AGREEMENT

BE IT KNOWN, for good consideration,

(First Party) and                                              (Second Party) being

parties to an original agreement having been dated                    , 19

(Agreement) which Agreement provides for:

Whereas said Agreement expires on                         , 19        , and the

parties desire to extend and continue said Agreement, it is provided that said Agreement

shall be extended and renewed for an additional term commencing upon the expiration of

the original term and expiring on                         , 19         .

This extension shall be on the same terms and conditions as contained in the

original Agreement all as if set forth and incorporated herein excepting only for the

following changes or modifications:

This extension of Agreement shall be binding upon and inure to the benefit of

the parties, their successors and assigns.

Signed under seal this                    day of                         , 19         .

In the presence of:

_____    _____

_____    _____

# AGREEMENT TO EXTEND PERFORMANCE DATE

BE IT KNOWN, for good consideration,

(First Party) and                                                              (Second Party) in and to

a certain agreement to:


dated                              , 19          (Agreement), do hereby acknowledge and agree that:

1.        Said Agreement provides that full performance on said agreement shall be

completed on or before                                        , 19      .

2.        That the parties acknowledge that said agreement cannot be performed and

completed on said date and that the parties hereupon desire to extend the performance

date.

3.        That the parties hereby mutually agree that the date for performance be

continued and extended to                                    , 19          , time being of the essence,

and there is no other change in terms or further extension allowed.

This Agreement shall be binding upon and inure to the benefit of the parties,

their successors and assigns.


Signed under seal this                              day of                                  , 19       .


In the presence of:


_____            _____


_____            _____

# MUTUAL CANCELLATION OF CONTRACT

BE IT KNOWN, for value received, that the undersigned being parties to a certain

contract dated            , 19    , whereas said contract provides for:

do hereby mutually cancel and terminate said contract effective this date.

We further provide that said termination shall be without further recourse by either

party against the other and this document shall constitute mutual releases of any further

obligations under said contract, all to the same extent as if said contract had not been

entered into in the first instance, provided the parties shall herewith undertake the below

described acts to terminate said contract, which obligations, if any, shall remain binding.

Signed under seal this         day of           , 19    .

_____

_____

# AFFIDAVIT

BE IT ACKNOWLEDGED, that                                    , the

undersigned deponent, being of legal age does hereby depose and say under oath as

follows (or as set forth on the signed addendum annexed and incorporated herein):

Witness my hand under the penalties of perjury this            day of

            , 19    .

_____

State of

            , SS.

County of                                                    , 19    .

Then personally appeared

who acknowledged the foregoing, before me.

_____

Notary Public

My Commission Expires:

# AFFIDAVIT OF LOST BOND OR STOCK CERTIFICATE

BE IT ACKNOWLEDGED, that the undersigned, being of lawful age, first being duly sworn, under oath states:

1.      That the undersigned is the lawful record owner of                    shares of the common stock or bonds of                                        (Corporation), as same appears on the books and records of the Corporation as certificate number(s) or bond number(s)                              . (Delete words that do not apply.)

2.      The undersigned has made a due and diligent search for said original stock certificate or bonds but has lost or misplaced same.  The undersigned warrants and represents that said stock certificate or bonds have not been sold, pledged or transferred, and shall be promptly returned to the Corporation if located.

3.      As an inducement for the Corporation issuing a duplicate replacement certificate, or bond, the undersigned agrees to fully indemnify and hold harmless the Corporation for any loss arising from any claim of ownership by any asserted owner or holder of said original shares or bond.

4.      Upon demand, the undersigned agrees to post bond for an amount equivalent to the value of said shares or bond or as reasonably may be required by Corporation.

Dated:

_____

State of
                                 , SS.
County of                                                      , 19      .

        Then personally appeared

who acknowledged the foregoing, before me.

_____
Notary Public

My Commission Expires:

# DIRECTION TO PAY

Date:

TO:_____

_____
Address

_____

Please be advised that you are hereby directed to pay to

_____

_____
Address

_____

The sum of $                          as is otherwise due me on the following

described account between us:

This direction to pay shall remain in full force and effect until further written notice

from me and you shall be duly credited for all payments so made in accordance with this

direction to pay.

Thank you for your cooperation in this matter.

_____
Name

_____
Address

_____

# PERMISSION TO USE QUOTE
# OR PERSONAL STATEMENT

BE IT KNOWN, for good consideration, the undersigned irrevocably and

unconditionally authorizes                                                                            ,

and its successors and assigns the worldwide rights to use, publish, print or reprint in

whole or in part the following statement, picture, endorsement, quotation or other material

attached or described as:


This authorization and rights hereto are _____ are not _____ exclusive.  This

authorization is _____ unlimited or _____ limited.  If limited, this authorization shall extend

only to a certain publication known as                                              ,

including all new editions, reprints, excerpts, advertisements, publicity and promotions

thereto of said work, and further including such publications as hold subsidiary rights

thereto, but shall not be published through any other medium.

The Undersigned acknowledges that the permission granted herein is non-

revocable, and that no further payment or consideration is due therein.

This agreement shall be binding upon and inure to the benefit of the parties, their

successors, assigns and personal representatives.


Signed under seal this              day of                              , 19        .


In the presence of:


_____          _____


                                                          _____

# PERMISSION TO USE
# COPYRIGHTED MATERIAL

BE IT KNOWN, for good consideration, the undersigned, as copyright holder,

hereby grants _____exclusive _____non-exclusive permission to

_____, to reprint, publish and use on its own account for world distribution

the following described material:

This copyright material shall be used only in the following manner:

A credit line to acknowledge permitted use of the material _____ is _____ is not

(check one) required. If required, the credit line shall read as follows:

This agreement shall be binding upon and inure to the benefit of the parties, their

successors, assigns and personal representatives.

Signed under seal this            day of                          , 19        .

In the presence of:

_____          _____
                                                                            Name


_____
                                                                            Address


_____

# REQUEST UNDER FREEDOM OF INFORMATION ACT

Date:

TO: _____

   Federal Agency

   _____

   Address

   _____

   Pursuant to the Federal Freedom of Information Act, I request disclosure of such information on me as may be maintained in your files, and to the extent said disclosure is required by law.

   Please forward said information to the address below.

   I appreciate your cooperation.

In the presence of:                  Very truly,


_____          _____
                                 Signature

                                 _____
                                 Name

                                 _____
                                 Other Known Names

                                 _____
                                 Address

                                 _____

                                 _____
                                 Social Security No.

# MAILING LIST
# NAME REMOVAL REQUEST

Date: _____

TO:_____
          Direct Mail Firm

_____
            Address

_____


Please be advised that I have received unsolicited mail from your firm, and I request that you remove my name from your mailing list, and not send me unsolicited material in the future.

My name and address appears as below (or as per mailing label attached):


_____
              Name

_____
          Street Address

_____
            City, State


Thank you for your attention to this request.



Very truly,



_____

# NOTICE OF ADDRESS CHANGE

Date: _____

TO:_____

_____
Address

_____

Please be advised that effective _____, 19_____ our address has been changed from

_____

_____

to

_____

_____

Our telephone number is

Please make note of the above information and direct all correspondence to us at our new address.

_____

# NOTICE OF ACCIDENT CLAIM

Date:

TO:_____

_____

Address

_____

You are hereby notified of a claim against you for damages arising from the following accident or injury.

Description of Accident:

Date:

Time:

Location:

Please have your insurance representative or attorney contact me as soon as possible.

Very truly,

_____

_____

Address

_____

# NOTICE OF CHANGE OF BENEFICIARY

Date:

TO:_____
Insurance Company

_____
Address

_____

BE IT ACKNOWLEDGED, that                    , is hereby designated beneficiary

in and to a certain life insurance policy numbered

issued by                              , said policy dated

19          and with a present death benefit payable in the amount of $

on the life of the undersigned.  This change of beneficiary acknowledgement terminates

all prior designations of beneficiary heretofore made.

Signed under seal this          day of                         , 19      .

_____
Insured

State of                                                   , 19      .
                    , SS.
County of

Then personally appeared

who acknowledged the foregoing, before me.

_____
Notary Public

My Commission Expires:

Accordingly, I name as new beneficiary                         of

. Please forward any necessary change of

beneficiary forms.

# NOTICE OF CHANGE OF LOSS PAYEE

Date:

TO:_____
              Insurance Company

_____
                  Address

_____

BE IT ACKNOWLEDGED, that                                    , is hereby

designated loss payee in and to a certain casualty insurance policy numbered

            , issued by                            , said policy dated

        , 19        , wherein the undersigned is named insured.  This change of

loss payee acknowledgement terminates all prior designations of loss payee heretofore

made, and you are to delete said party as loss payee.

        Signed under seal this        day of                    , 19      .


                                    _____
                                    Insured


State of                                                    , 19      .
                    , SS.
County of

        Then personally appeared

who acknowledged the foregoing, before me.


                                    _____
                                    Notary Public

                                    My Commission Expires:

# NOTICE OF INSURANCE CLAIM

Date:

TO:_____
                    Insurer

_____
                    Address

_____

You are hereby notified that we have incurred a loss covered by insurance to which you are the underwriter. The claim information is as follows:

1.   Type of Loss or Claim:

2.   Date Incurred:

3.   Location:

4.   Estimated Loss or Casualty:

   Please forward a claim form or have an adjuster call (          ) -

   Very truly,

_____          _____
Policy Number                              Name

                                           _____
                                           Address

# NOTICE OF PRODUCT DEFECT CLAIM

Date:

TO:_____
       Manufacturer, Supplier or Seller

_____
              Address

_____

Notice is hereby provided that we have purchased a product manufactured,

distributed or sold by you and described as:

You are advised us of a product defect or warranty claim in the following

particulars:

Date of Purchase:

Nature of Reported Defect:

Reported Injuries or Damage:

Purchased From:

This letter is provided to give you earliest possible notice of said claim, and we

request that you or your representative contact us as soon as possible.

We shall advise you upon receipt of any further information on this claim.

Very truly,

_____

CERTIFIED MAIL, Return Receipt Requested

# NOTICE OF PRODUCT WARRANTY CLAIM

Date:

TO:_____

_____
                Address

_____

Gentlemen:

Please be advised that we purchased the following product

                                        , from

        , on                        , 19      .

This product is defective and in need of repair in the following particulars:

We understand that this product is under warranty and we therefore request

repair of the product under warranty.

_____  Product enclosed

_____  Please call (                        ) for a service appointment.

Very truly,

_____

_____
                Address

_____

# NOTICE OF BREACH OF CONTRACT

Date:

TO:_____

_____
Address

_____

Reference is made to a certain agreement between us dated

19    which agreement provides that:

PLEASE TAKE NOTICE that you are in breach of your obligations under said

contract in the following particulars:

You are further advised that we shall hold you responsible for all actual and

consequential damages arising from your breach.

_____

_____
Address

_____

# GENERAL RELEASE

BE IT KNOWN, for good consideration, that the undersigned hereby jointly and severally forever releases, discharges, acquits and forgives

from any and all claims, actions, suits, demands, agreements, liabilities and proceedings of every nature and description both at law and in equity arising from the beginning of time to the date of these presence and more particularly related to an incident or claim that arose out of:

This release shall be binding upon and inure to the benefit of the parties, their successors, assigns and personal representatives.

Signed under seal this                    day of                         , 19      .

Witnessed:

_____          _____


_____          _____

# MUTUAL RELEASES

BE IT KNOWN, for good consideration, and in further consideration of the mutual releases herein entered into, that:

(First Party) and

(Second Party) do hereby completely, mutually and reciprocally release, discharge, acquit and forgive each other from all claims, contracts, actions, suits, demands, agreements, liabilities and proceedings of every nature and description both at law and in equity that either party has or may have against the other, arising from the beginning of time to the date of these presence, including but not necessarily limited to an incident or claim arising from:

This release shall be binding upon and inure to the benefit of the parties, their successors, assigns and personal representatives.

Signed under seal this                    day of                    , 19        .

In the presence of:

_____        _____

_____        _____

# SPECIFIC RELEASE

BE IT KNOWN, for good consideration, the undersigned jointly and severally

hereby forever releases, discharges and acquits

from any and all contracts, claims, suits, actions or liabilities both in law and in equity

specifically arising from, relating to or otherwise described as and limited to:

This release applies only to the foregoing matters and extends to no other debt,

account, agreement, obligations, cause of action, liability or undertaking by and between

the parties, which, if existing, shall survive this release and remain in full force and effect

and undisturbed by this specific release.

This release shall be binding upon and inure to the benefit of the parties, their

successors, assigns and personal representatives.

Signed under seal this                    day of                         , 19        .

Witnessed:

_____    _____


_____    _____

# RELEASE OF CLAIMS — HUSBAND AND WIFE

BE IT KNOWN, for good consideration, that the undersigned as husband and

wife hereby jointly and severally forever release, discharge, acquit and forgive

from any and all claims, actions, suits, demands, agreements, liabilities and proceedings

of every nature and description both at law and in equity arising from the beginning of time

to the date of these presence and more particularly related to an incident or claim that

arose out of:

This release shall be binding upon and inure to the benefit of the parties, their

successors, assigns and personal representatives.

Signed under seal this                    day of                         , 19      .

Witnessed:

_____          _____
                                     Husband

_____          _____
                                     Wife

# RELEASE OF PERSONAL INJURY CLAIM

BE IT KNOWN, that in consideration of the sum of $                    , here-

with paid, I,                                    of

                          , do hereby release, discharge, forgive

and acquit                                    from any further claim, action,

suit or liability in connection with a certain personal injury claim arising from:

The undersigned acknowledges that it may have further medical bills or future

injuries or disability and the extent of injuries are presently unknown, but that said factors

have been duly taken into consideration in the issuance of this release.

This release shall be binding upon and inure to the benefit of the parties, their

successors, assigns and personal representatives.

Signed under seal this            day of                          , 19        .

_____

# COVENANT NOT TO SUE

BE IT KNOWN, for good consideration, the undersigned being the holder of an actual, existing, asserted or prospective claim against

arising from or relative to:

do hereby covenant that I/we shall not commence, maintain or prosecute any suit thereon against said party whether at law or in equity provided nothing herein shall constitute a release of this or any other party thereto and I expressly reserve all rights against any third parties.

Further, the payment of any consideration hereunder shall not constitute an admission of liability by covenantee or any third party. There are no promises or inducements except as herein contained.

This covenant shall be binding upon and shall inure to the benefit of the parties, their successors, assigns and personal representatives.

Signed under seal this                    day of                              , 19   .

In the presence of:

_____          _____

_____          _____

# PROXY TO VOTE CORPORATE SHARES

BE IT KNOWN, that the undersigned, being the owner of                    shares

of voting common stock of                                        (Corporation)

do hereby grant to                                   a proxy and appoint him my

attorney-in-fact to vote on behalf of the undersigned              shares of said stock

at any future general or special meeting of the stockholders of the Corporation, and said

proxyholder is entitled to attend said meetings and act on my behalf and vote said shares

personally or through mail proxy, all to the same extent as if I voted said shares personally.

During the pendency of this proxy, all rights to vote said shares shall be held by

the proxyholder with full power of substitution or revocation, provided the undersigned

may revoke this proxy at any time, upon written notice of termination by certifed mail,

return receipt to both the proxyholder and corporation.

The proxyholder shall be entitled to reimbursement for reasonable expenses

incurred hereunder, but otherwise shall not be entitled to compensation for the services

to be rendered.

This agreement shall be binding upon and inure to the benefit of the parties, their

successors, assigns and personal representatives.

IN WITNESS WHEREOF, I have executed this proxy this              day of

              , 19        .

Accepted:

_____          _____
Proxyholder                               Stockholder


State of                                                        , 19        .
                        , SS.
County of

Then personally appeared

who acknowledged the foregoing, before me.


_____
Notary Public

My Commission Expires:

# AUTHORIZATION TO RELEASE
# CONFIDENTIAL INFORMATION

Date:

TO:_____

_____
Address

_____

You are hereby authorized and directed to mail or deliver to:

_____

_____
Address

_____

either original or copies of the below described documents or confidential information that

you may have in your possession.

You may bill me for any costs associated with your compliance with this request and I

thank you for your cooperation.

Very truly,

_____

_____
Address

_____

# SUBMISSION OF UNSOLICITED IDEAS

Date:

TO:_____

_____
Address

_____

Thank you for your interest in submitting for our consideration an idea or proposal described as:


As you can understand, our company receives many commercial ideas, suggestions and proposals, and also has many of its own projects under development. Therefore, the idea or proposal you plan to submit to us may have been considered and/or may already be in the planning or development stages.

Accordingly, we would be pleased to accept your idea or proposal for review, on condition you acknowledge: 1. Samples or other submissions will be returned only if return postage or freight is prepaid; 2. The company accepts no responsibility for casualty or loss to samples or other submitted material in our possession; 3. The company accepts no responsibility for holding any submitted information in confidence; 4. The company shall pay compensation only in the event it, (a) accepts the submitted idea, (b) has received the idea exclusively from you, and (c) reaches agreement with you as to terms and conditions, for development of the product or exploitation of the idea.

If these terms are acceptable to you, please sign where indicated below and submit with your idea or proposal. We shall thereafter advise you of our interest.

Acknowledged:


_____          _____

# GUARANTY OF CONTRACT

FOR GOOD CONSIDERATION, the undersigned (Guarantor) does hereby

guaranty to                                        the full, prompt and complete performance

by                                        of all the terms, conditions and covenants

of a contract between them hereto annexed and dated                        , 19        .

This guaranty shall continue until all the terms and conditions of said contract

have been fully performed and the Guarantor shall not be released of any obligation or

liability hereunder so long as there is any claim or right of claim arising out of said contract.

In the event of any claimed breach of contract the Guarantor shall be afforded  full right to

perform said obligations thereunder.  There shall be no modification of said contract

without the assent of Guarantor.  This guaranty shall be unlimited as to duration or

amount.

This guaranty shall be binding upon and inure to the benefit of the parties their

successors, assigns and personal representatives.


Signed under seal this                day of                        , 19        .


_____

# INDIVIDUAL ACKNOWLEDGEMENT

State of

                     , SS.

County of

On the        day of                 , 19      , before me personally

came                        , to me known to be the individual

described in and who executed the document annexed hereto and who executed the

same in my presence or acknowledged said signature as a true and free act and deed,

before me.

_____

Notary Public

My Commission Expires:

# CORPORATE ACKNOWLEDGEMENT

State of

, SS.

County of

On the          day of                          , 19       , before me personally

came                                              , who being by me duly sworn,

did depose and say that he is the                          of

, the corporation described in and which executed the

annexed document; that he knows the seal of said corporation; that the seal affixed is

such corporate seal; that it was so affixed by order of the Board of Directors of said

corporation, and that he signed his name thereto by like order.

_____

Notary Public

My Commission Expires:

# PARTNERSHIP ACKNOWLEDGEMENT

State of

                           , SS.

County of

On the       day of                  , 19     , before me personally appeared                         , known to me, or proved to me on the basis of satisfactory evidence to be one of the partnership that executed the within instrument, and acknowledged to me that said partnership executed the same.

_____
Notary Public

My Commission Expires:

# ATTORNEY-IN-FACT ACKNOWLEDGEMENT

State of

, SS.

County of


On the          day of                          , 19      , personally appeared

, known to me or proved to me on the

basis of satisfactory evidence to be the person whose name is subscribed to the within

instrument as the attorney-in-fact of                                        , and

acknowledged to me that he subscribed the name of

thereto as principal, and his own name as authorized attorney-in-fact.


_____

Notary Public

My Commission Expires:

# WILL-MAKER
# AND
# ESTATE PLANNING
# GUIDE

10

# WILL-MAKER &

# ESTATE PLANNING GUIDE

---

In just a few moments you can protect your family and avoid serious problems by preparing a legally valid will.

Prepared by a team of lawyers, Will-Maker allows you to draw your own will quickly, safely and easily and without costly legal fees.

A will is perhaps the most important legal document you and your family will ever rely upon. Without a valid will the state - not you - decides who will inherit your property. Moreover, you forfeit the right to decide who will represent your estate and more importantly, who will serve as guardian of your minor children.

Regardless of the size of your estate, failing to make a will, or periodically update and make a new will, means taking needless chances.

Within the Will-Maker and Estate Planning Guide you have all the information you will ordinarily require to prepare your own will. Read the instructions carefully and if you remain uncertain on how to complete your will or if you have complex legal situations not adequately covered by this guide, you should seek legal assistance.

*" This publication is designed to provide accurate and authoritative information in regard to the subject matter covered. It is sold with the understanding that the publisher is not engaged in rendering legal, accounting or other professional service. If legal advice or other expert assistance is required, the services of a competent professional person should be sought."*

From a Declaration of Principles jointly adopted by a Committee of the American Bar Association and a Committee of Publishers and Associations.

# PREPARING YOUR WILL

### Preliminary Instructions:

Be certain to type or write your will in ink. Do not cross out words or make erasures. Writing a draft copy in advance can help you avoid mistakes. If you want copies of your will they should be made before you sign the original.

### Name and Address:

Complete the will using your full name as it generally appears on legal documents. The correct address (City, County and State) is important because it identifies the Court in which the will should be probated.

### Executor:

You must name an executor for your estate and authorize your executor to probate your estate and carry out the provisions of your will. Typically a spouse, relative or close friend serves as executor as the duties of an executor are not difficult and your executor will usually retain an attorney to process the necessary probate forms. The primary concerns in selecting an executor is that he or she be reliable and trustworthy in carrying out your specific wishes. Only Nevada requires the executor to be from within the state. In all other states you may appoint a non-resident, provided he or she is of lawful age. Always check with your proposed executor in advance to be certain he or she is willing to serve, and name an alternate executor in the event the named executor shall, for any reason, be unable to serve.

### Guardian:

If you have minor children or dependents you should name a guardian to care for said children or dependents in the event you leave them without another parent. Since a guardian takes the place of a parent you will want an individual who can offer the best care for your children or dependents, which in most cases will be a close relative willing to accept the responsibility. As with your executor, you should name an alternate guardian if the primary guardian cannot serve.

### Special Bequests:

Bequests should always be clear, complete and specific as to who is to receive what property.

Examples:

*I give my 1987 Chevrolet Caprice to my son David Smith.*

or

*I bequeath to the First Baptist Church of Sioux City the sum of $10,000 to use in any manner they deem proper.*

Your special bequest should also indicate whether the property is to be gifted subject to mortgages or encumbrances against it, or whether it is to be gifted free and clear, with any debts against the property paid from your general estate.

Examples:

> *I leave to my daughter Jane Smith my home at 10 Elm Street,
> Sioux City, subject to all mortgages.*

> or

> *I leave to my dear friend Harry Bennett my 1986 Sea Ray Sedan
> Cruiser, free of all encumbrances.*

## Forgiveness of Debts:

Under a will you may release a person from obligation to repay monies owed you. If a person you release from a debt is a beneficiary, you should state whether they are to receive their full bequest or whether the debt is to be deducted.

Example:

> *I leave $100,000 to my nephew William Smith, less such balance
> on the $10,000 loan that he then owes me.*

## Disinheritence:

You may wish to disinherit a child or spouse who would otherwise have a claim on your estate if you had no will, or if your will should be declared invalid.

You can lawfully disinherit a child, however it is important you specifically mention the child and your intention to disinherit. If you simply omit mention of a child the law presumes you forgot the child and entitles the child to his or her statutory share as if you died without a will (intestate). Proper language to disinherit may read, for example:

> *Since I have not heard from my son James Smith in over ten years,
> I leave him nothing.*

> or

> *I recognize my daughter  Marilyn Smith is financially secure, and
> therefore leave her nothing.*

In many states it is impossible to completely disinherit a spouse as the spouse would nevertheless be entitled to the same share as if you died without a will. If it is your intention to disinherit your spouse but are uncertain of the laws of your state, you may use this language as an example:

> *I leave to my wife Mildred, absolutely nothing or if unlawful to do so,
> such minimum share of my estate as shall be required by state law.*

Remember, it is often wise to leave your children and spouse some bequest so as to avoid a contest over your will.

## Residuary Bequests:

The "residuary" clause states who will receive the remainder of your estate, other than specific bequests. You may wish to avoid specific bequests altogether in which case your will shall only contain a residuary bequest.

If your will contains no specific bequests the residuary clause may read:

*I leave all my property to my wife Clara Jones.*

If there are specific bequests it would read:

*I leave all the rest of my property to my wife Clara Jones.*

## Contingent Beneficiaries:

It is possible that a named beneficiary may predecease you in which event you should name a contingent or alternate beneficiary.

Example:

*I leave all my property to my wife Clara Jones but if she shall predecease me I leave said property to The First Baptist Church of Sioux City.*

## Signing the Will:

You may prepare the will in advance of signing it, however, you must sign the will in the presence of your witnesses.  Sign with your full name as it appears on the first page of the will.  If additional will pages are required, sign each additional page along the margin.

## Witnesses:

The most important point in making sure your will is valid is to have it properly witnessed.  Most states require two (2) witnesses, but Vermont, New Hampshire and South Carolina each require three (3) witnesses.  It may nevertheless be a good idea in all states to use three (3) witnesses in the event a witness becomes disqualified.

Witnesses must be disinterested parties and therefore cannot be named in the will as beneficiary, executor or guardian.

You must sign in the presence of the witnesses, and the witnesses should then sign in your presence and in the presence of each other.  Remember, neither you nor any witness should leave the room until the will is both signed and witnessed.

## Safekeeping Your Will:

Keep your will in a safe, secure location and notify your executor of the location as he or she will need it to probate your estate.  Do not keep it in a safe deposit box as some states seal a box upon death.

## Revising Your Will:

It is good practice to review and if necessary revise your will every two or three years.  Events that usually warrant preparing a new will include:  moving to another state, divorce or marriage, family additions, the desire to change beneficiaries or a major change in your financial condition.

If your will needs major revision, simply write a new one and, once completed, destroy your prior will.

# LAST WILL AND TESTAMENT

## OF

_____

I,                                , a resident of
County of                        , in the State of
being of sound mind, do make and declare this to be my Last Will and Testament
expressly revoking all my prior wills and codicils at any time made.

## I.    EXECUTOR:

I appoint                         as Executor of this my Last Will and
Testament and provide if this Executor is unable or unwilling to serve then I appoint
                 as alternate Executor. My Executor shall be authorized
to carry out all provisions of this Will and pay my just debts, obligations and funeral
expenses. I further provide my Executor shall not be required to post surety bond in this
or any other jurisdiction, and direct that no expert appraisal be made of my estate unless
required by law.

## II.    GUARDIAN:

In the event I shall die as the sole parent of minor children, then I appoint
                 Guardian of said minor children. If this named Guardian is
unable or unwilling to serve, then I appoint                      as
alternate Guardian.

## III.    BEQUESTS:

IN WITNESS WHEREOF, I have hereunto set my hand this                    day of
                , 19       .


_____
Signature


_____


IV.     __WITNESSED__:

        This Last Will and Testament of                                         was
signed and declared to be his/her Last Will and Testament in our presence and at his/her
request and in his/her presence and in the presence of each other, we do hereby witness
same on this                    day of                                 , 19       .


_____          _____
Witness Signature                      Address


_____          _____
Witness Signature                      Address


_____          _____
Witness Signature                      Address

# PERSONAL INFORMATION

FULL LEGAL NAME _____

ADDRESS _____

S.S. NO. _____  SPOUSE _____

MEDICARE NO. _____  SPOUSE _____

ARMED FORCES SERVICE NO. _____

DATE & LOCATION OF DISCHARGE _____

BIRTH DATE _____  MARRIAGE DATE _____

FATHER'S FULL NAME _____

MOTHER'S FULL MAIDEN NAME _____

WIDOWED ___ SEPARATED ___ DIVORCED ___ DATE _____

LOCATION OF SEPARATION AGREEMENT/DIVORCE DECREE _____

_____

REMARRIED? YES ___ NO ___          DATE _____

CHILDREN FROM PREVIOUS MARRIAGE(S)? YES ___ NO ___

LIST:

| NAME | ADDRESS | BIRTH DATE |
|------|---------|------------|
| _____ | _____ | _____ |
| _____ | _____ | _____ |
| _____ | _____ | _____ |

## WILL

LOCATION OF ORIGINAL LAST WILL_____

_____DATE _____

CODICIL COMPLETED? YES ___ NO ___ IF YES, LOCATION _____

_____ DATE _____

LOCATION OF ANY DOCUMENTS MENTIONED IN WILL _____

_____ DATE _____

# NOTIFICATION LIST

| Relatives & Friends Full Name | Address | Telephone |
|---|---|---|
| _____ | _____ | _____ |
| _____ | _____ | _____ |
| _____ | _____ | _____ |

ACCOUNTANT _____

_____

ATTORNEY_____

_____

BANKER_____

_____

CLERGYMAN _____

_____

EXECUTOR _____

_____

CONTINGENT EXECUTOR _____

_____

FUNERAL DIRECTOR _____

_____

GUARDIAN _____

_____

CONTINGENT GUARDIAN _____

_____

INSURANCE AGENT _____

_____

INSURANCE UNDERWRITER _____

_____

# FUNERAL ARRANGEMENTS

FUNERAL HOME/PLAN _____

DIRECTOR _____ TELEPHONE _____

ADDRESS _____

SERVICE TYPE:  RELIGIOUS _____  MILITARY _____  FRATERNAL _____

PERSON OFFICIATING _____ TELEPHONE _____

MUSIC SELECTIONS _____

READING SELECTIONS _____

FLOWERS _____

MEMORIALS _____

PALLBEARERS _____

TELEPHONE NOS. _____

DISPOSITION:          BURIAL _____          CREMATION _____

OTHER INSTRUCTIONS _____

## BURIAL

CEMETARY _____

LOCATION _____

SECTION _____ PLOT NO. _____ BLOCK _____

LOCATION OF DEED _____

SPECIAL INSTRUCTIONS _____

## FUNERAL EXPENSES COVERAGE

LIFE INSURANCE _____

SOCIAL SECURITY _____VETERAN'S ADMINISTRATION _____

UNION BENEFIT _____ FRATERNAL ORGANIZATION(S) _____

PENSION BENEFIT _____

BURIAL INSURANCE _____

MILITARY _____

# INSURANCE/PENSION DATA

## LIFE INSURANCE POLICIES

COMPANY _____

AGENT _____ PHONE _____

POLICY NUMBER _____ DATE _____

AMOUNT_____ OWNER _____

LOCATION OF POLICY _____

BENEFICIARY _____

COMPANY _____

AGENT _____ PHONE _____

POLICY NUMBER _____ DATE _____

AMOUNT _____ OWNER _____

LOCATION OF POLICY _____

BENEFICIARY _____

COMPANY _____

AGENT _____ PHONE _____

POLICY NUMBER _____ DATE _____

AMOUNT _____ OWNER _____

LOCATION OF POLICY _____

BENEFICIARY _____

## PENSIONS/ANNUITIES

COMPANY _____

CONTACT _____ PHONE _____

AGREEMENT NO. _____ DATE _____

AMOUNT _____ OWNER _____

LOCATION OF AGREEMENT_____

# DOCUMENT LOCATOR

Insurance Documents:_____

Birth Certificate:_____

Letters of Instruction in Case of Death: _____

Deeds and Proof of Ownership: _____

Marriage License or Certificate:_____

Social Security Cards: _____

Military Records: _____

Divorce Decree:_____

Mortgage Documents: _____

Bank Passbooks:_____

Passport(s):_____

Tax Returns:_____

Will(s) and Trust(s):_____

Prenuptial Agreement:_____

Business Papers: _____

Death Certificates: _____

Warranties: _____

Stock Certificates: _____

Other Investment Certificates: _____

Letters of Final Request: _____

Anatomical Gift Authorization:_____

Citizenship Papers: _____

Safe Deposit Keys: _____

Financial Records: _____